1978

MILTON'S SAMSON

AND THE CHRISTIAN TRADITION

Milton's Samson
and the Christian Tradition

By F. Michael Krouse

OCTAGON BOOKS

A DIVISION OF FARRAR, STRAUS AND GIROUX

New York 1974

Title page decoration is from
Benedictus Arias Montanus, *De Varia Republica* (Antwerp, 1592)
Courtesy of Union Theological Seminary

Reprinted 1974
by special arrangement with Princeton University Press

OCTAGON BOOKS
A DIVISION OF FARRAR, STRAUS & GIROUX, INC.
19 Union Square West
New York, N. Y. 10003

Library of Congress Cataloging in Publication Data

Krouse, F. Michael.
    Milton's Samson and the Christian tradition.

    Reprint of the ed. published by Princeton University Press, Prince-
ton, which was a revision and expansion of the author's dissertation, John Hopkins University, 1946.

    Bibliography: p.

    1. Milton, John, 1608-1670. Samson Agonistes.   2. Samson, judge
of Israel, in fiction, drama, poetry, etc.   I. Title.
[PR3566.K7   1974]   821'.4   74-762
ISBN 0-374-94651-5

Printed in U.S.A. by
NOBLE OFFSET PRINTERS, INC.
New York, N.Y. 10003

FOR

John Townley Krouse

Preface

MORE than twenty years ago Professor Allan H. Gilbert remarked in a review that we could never hope to understand *Samson Agonistes* until the play had been studied in the light of the biblical commentaries from which Milton might have derived many of his conceptions. Although it will surprise, and may disappoint, Professor Gilbert, this book tries to follow his suggestion. It is to him ultimately that I am indebted for the subject of this study.

I have tried to acknowledge numerous debts to many other writers in the notes and the bibliography, but I owe much to several persons whose aid was such as is not revealed by documentary apparatus. Professor Don Cameron Allen has aided me with guidance, encouragement, and friendship since 1944, when I first set to work to prepare a doctoral dissertation on this subject at the Johns Hopkins University. At that time, too, Professor Raymond D. Havens criticized the earliest version of my manuscript with characteristic thoroughness, insight, and loving-kindness. Professors Ludwig Edelstein, H. Carrington Lancaster, and John B. McDiarmid gave me valuable assistance, always with the generosity and courtesy of true humanists. I am grateful to them and to my fellow-students during those years for making it possible for me to do this work in the happiest possible circumstances. I am particularly indebted to Dr. Ernest S. Gohn for calling my attention to many references to Samson and for his sustained interest in this project, and to Professor Elizabeth Marie Pope, now of Mills College, whose study of *Paradise Regained* convinced me that we can be good readers of Milton today only by acquainting ourselves with the now-forgotten tradition which he expected his readers to know.

Since I undertook to revise, rewrite, and expand this study for publication in book form, I have received much help from colleagues in the McMicken College of Liberal Arts at the University of Cincinnati, especially from Professor Alister

Cameron, who helped in the checking of the Greek quotations in Chapter VI. I wish to express my gratitude to Professors Robert Shafer and Malcolm Francis McGregor for all they have done to protect Alcmena from Juno, and to the Faculty Committee and Trustees of the Charles Phelps Taft Memorial Fund for the generous aid which has made publication possible. Professor Maurice Kelley of Princeton University gave me aid of a most generous sort, both in criticizing the manuscript and in reading the galley proofs.

My wife—"Angelus unicuique suus . . . obtigit aethereis ales ab ordinibus"—has been a partner in this enterprise, as in all. The extent of her interest is suggested, though not comprehended, by the fact that she has typed the manuscript twice.

I sincerely appreciate the kindness which I have encountered at all times in using the collections of the libraries of the Johns Hopkins University, Yale University, Union Theological Seminary, the Peabody Institute, the University of Cincinnati, and the University of Chicago, and of the New York Public Library, the Library of Congress, and the Folger Shakespeare Library.

If this book has great faults, the friends who tried to save it from error and the many writers on whose contributions it leans are not to blame.

F. M. K.

McMicken College of Liberal Arts
The University of Cincinnati

Contents

Illustrations

MILTON'S SAMSON
AND THE CHRISTIAN TRADITION

Chapter I

INTRODUCTORY: *SAMSON AGONISTES* AND THE CRITICS

THERE has often been an undercurrent of disparagement in what critics have said about Milton's *Samson Agonistes*. When Bishop Hurd called it "the most artificial and highly finished of all Milton's poetical works," he was praising the poem but faintly: even in the eighteenth century, poems of pure art, like men of pure genius, were more often admired than loved. One is not surprised to learn from Professor Havens' study of Milton's influence that *Samson Agonistes* has seldom been imitated. It has been widely admired as a *tour de force*, certain features of it have been highly praised, several critics have considered it Milton's greatest work, and yet very few have ever taken it to their hearts. Mr. Tillyard, for one, has confessed that *Samson Agonistes* appeals to him least of the three major poems of Milton and has even suggested that the tragedy is worth preserving only because it is a remarkable personal document of an important poet.

Scholars have often been moved to contrive historical or other defenses for works which critics have depreciated solely on aesthetic ground, and in our own time this impulse to defend old writings against adverse criticism has sometimes produced convincing revaluations of those writings. But as yet no such revaluation of *Samson Agonistes* has been accomplished; indeed, Milton's tragedy has been studied surprisingly little and rather superficially. It has never received the close attention lavished upon *Paradise Lost*, or *The Faerie Queene*, or even the least prepossessing plays of Shakespeare.

Because the critics have either neglected *Samson Agonistes* or taken it for granted, one may still say of it what Sir Walter Raleigh once said of *Paradise Lost*: it is "a monument to dead ideas." By attempting to do no more than read this poem from the point of view of our own day, we have had to content ourselves with reading it badly. *Samson Agonistes*, like every other poem from a past age, contains, and is built upon, the thinking of a day that is gone. Much of that thinking is hidden in what Professor Lovejoy called "implicit assumptions." It is these unknown and unsuspected dead ideas which must be disinterred, identified, and raised like Lazarus if we are interested in reading those poems as the poet meant them to be read. Most of our traditions have changed greatly during the past three hundred years, and many traditions have, in that interval, been altogether lost and forgotten. Such silent and concealed changes greatly affect our understanding and evaluation of writings as old as Milton's *Samson Agonistes* because, as a pair of English critics have observed, "value in any art depends on the interaction of an individual creative will and a valid tradition," and for this reason "three-quarters of our study must always be the attempt to reacquire the traditional content of the imagination."[1]

It is this attempt to reacquire the traditional content of the imagination of Milton and his contemporary public that critics have failed to make in connection with *Samson Agonistes*. They have probed for sources, anatomized its dramatic structure, traced its relationship to Greek drama, speculated about the poet's reasons for choosing Samson as a subject for tragedy, tried to extract political and social satire or autobiographical revelation from it, and analyzed its characters. But, since all this has been done without reference to the tradition with which Milton's creative will worked, our present conception of the meaning of *Samson Agonistes* and of its value as poetry is still open to question and to possible modification or abandonment when once it is reviewed against the backdrop of that tradition.

This study of Milton's Samson in the light of the Christian tradition will attempt to re-weave a piece of this backdrop from the numerous, scattered threads of it which have been

---

[1] W. L. Renwick and Harold Orton, *The Beginnings of English Literature* (New York, 1940), p. 24.

preserved. But, before this purpose is more clearly and specifi-
cally stated, it is desirable that one have freshly in mind the
assumptions about Milton's tragedy to which we have thus
far been led by scholarship and criticism. The second section
of this chapter is meant to reveal these assumptions by sur-
veying the criticism of *Samson Agonistes* up to the present
time; the final section of this chapter suggests a new direction
of study and defines a particular problem in that direction.

2

EVER since the appearance of the earliest critical editions of
Samson Agonistes, Milton's readers have been made aware
of a vast number of references and allusions to biblical and
classical literature imbedded in the poem. Most of the edi-
torial acumen expended on *Samson Agonistes* has been devoted to such details. Newton perceived many sources, parallels, and analogues, especially in the Greek tragic poets and
in Hesiod, Vergil, Seneca, Horace, and Ovid.[2] His conception of sources is typical of the eighteenth- and nineteenth-

---

[2] Thomas Newton's *Poetical Works of John Milton* (London, 1749-
1761) was the earliest critical edition of all the poetry of Milton in which
Samson Agonistes was fully annotated. The earlier edition by Patrick Hume
(1695) contained no critical notes to *Samson Agonistes*. Henry J. Todd's
great variorum edition, *The Poetical Works of John Milton* (London,
1801), is more than just a storehouse of eighteenth-century Miltonic criticism, for Todd's own notes advanced the study of Milton appreciably
beyond the stage which it had reached in the period of Warburton. In
the latter part of the nineteenth century David Masson's *Poetical Works of
John Milton* (London, 1874-1890) contained excellent notes to *Samson
Agonistes*; and in the same era separate editions of the poems with elaborate
critical apparatus began to appear. The first of these was the edition of
A. J. Church (London, 1872), followed by that of H. M. Perceval (London, 1890), and that of A. W. Verity (Cambridge, 1912). The best recent
critical edition of *Samson Agonistes* is that of Merritt Y. Hughes (New
York, 1937). The editors have perceived no serious textual difficulties in
this tragedy. The *editio princeps* (*Paradise Regain'd, a Poem in IV Books,
to Which is Added Samson Agonistes* [London, 1671]) is the only edition
known to have appeared during Milton's lifetime. That edition is the basis
of the text of the poem in *The Works of John Milton* (the Columbia
edition), ed. F. A. Patterson (New York, 1931-1938), I, 329 *et seq.*, and
of the same editor's *The Student's Milton*, revised edition (New York,
1933). Throughout the present book all quotations from Milton are taken
from the Columbia edition.

century editors: scholars in search of sources have always
found what they wanted in the books which they happened
to know well. Todd seems to have been the first to look
beyond that part of Graeco-Roman literature known to every
schoolboy in the England of his day to suggest that some
features of *Samson Agonistes* not traceable to the Book of
Judges itself might have resulted from Milton's acquaintance
with the *Jewish Antiquities* of Josephus, although, to be sure,
Charles Dunster had argued, just before the appearance of
Todd's edition, that *Paradise Lost* was indebted to Sylvester's
translation of Du Bartas.[3] Southey extended the range of
sources in 1825 by suggesting that Milton had borrowed from
the seventeenth-century Dutch poet, Joost van den Vondel,[4]
and George Edmundson later urged that Milton was indebted
to Vondel in all three major poems, but especially in *Samson
Agonistes*.[5] Francis Quarles' *Historie of Samson* (1632) has
sometimes been mentioned as a possible source for Milton's
tragedy, but Milton's critics have almost unanimously concluded that there was little or nothing in Quarles' prolix work
which could have moved Milton to emulation or yielded him
inspiration.[6] Most critics—even those engaged in pressing the
claims of one or another literary precursor—have agreed that
the principal source of *Samson Agonistes* is the account of
Samson in the Book of Judges,[7] although Professor Hanford

[3] *Considerations on Milton's Early Reading* (London, 1800), p. 11f.
[4] Verity, ed., *Milton's "Samson Agonistes"* (Cambridge, Mass., 1932),
p. 158. Edmund Gosse perpetuated Southey's conjecture in *Studies in the
Literature of Northern Europe* (London, 1883), pp. 278-312.
[5] *Milton and Vondel: a Curiosity of Literature* (London, 1885), esp.
pp. 158-92. Edmundson's argument has since been demolished by Verity
(*op.cit.*, pp. 158-68) and by H. J. C. Grierson ("A Note upon the *Samson
Agonistes* of John Milton and *Samson of Heilige Wraeck* by Joost van den
Vondel," in *Mélanges . . . Baldensperger* [Paris, 1930], pp. 1-8. See also
Jehangir R. P. Mody, *Vondel and Milton* (Bombay, 1942) and the review
by Helen Darbishire (*RES*, XIX, 330).
[6] See, for example, Verity, p. xxix. The opposite view has been expressed rather recently by George W. Whiting, *Milton's Literary Milieu*
(Chapel Hill, 1939), pp. 252-59.
[7] This was Verity's contention (p. xxvii). W. R. Parker, in *Milton's
Debt to Greek Tragedy in "Samson Agonistes"* (Baltimore, 1937), ch. I,
asserts that nearly everything in Milton's drama can be traced to Greek

once urged that Milton was heavily indebted to the Book of Job for the essentials of his conception of Samson's character.[8] More than a century of hue and cry after sources has resulted in disappointingly little enrichment of the poem for the modern reader. Even when the pursuit has run in the direction of the Old Testament itself, the pursuer has assumed that Milton read his Bible very much as those do who read it today: in a vacuum, without any accretion of interpretation, of tradition. But Milton had no Bible designed to be "read as living literature," nor can we suppose that he would have welcomed such a work. It would not have occurred to him to read either Job or Judges simply as a poem devoid of religious significance; yet the search for sources has always assumed that he did something like that. No wonder it has yielded so little genuine understanding of the tragedy. When all the allusions have been run down and all conceivable indebtednesses have been projected, we are left with further evidence of Milton's omnivorousness as a reader and with an even greater feeling of awe before the artist who created so sublime a work with such meager raw materials. It is fortunate for the quality of Miltonic criticism as a whole, and of the criticism of *Samson Agonistes* in particular, that source-hunting has never got the upper hand. The best of Milton's critics have more often given their attention to other problems.

The only other critical approach to *Samson Agonistes* hallowed by as much time as the study of sources is the analysis of its dramatic structure, an approach which has been equally fruitless and indecisive. Bishop Atterbury's suggestion that Pope adapt the poem for the stage indicates that the Augustans were not satisfied with the poem as drama.[9] But this dissatisfaction was not made entirely explicit until Dr. Johnson (*Rambler*, no. 139) declared that the plot of this poem,

---

tragedy, to Judges, to the poet's own experience, and to "a moderate exercise of dramatic invention."

[8] "*Samson Agonistes* and Milton in Old Age," in *Studies in Shakespeare, Milton, and Donne* (New York, 1925), p. 174.

[9] R. D. Havens, *The Influence of Milton on English Poetry* (Cambridge, Mass., 1922), p. 117 and n. 2. See also Newton, *op.cit.*, III, 305.

"which ignorance has admired, and bigotry applauded," lacks a middle. This censure and the line of criticism which has followed it is already so familiar to Miltonists that little need be said about it here. Richard Cumberland wrote a spirited and rather effective reply to Johnson in the *Observer*, arguing that the bearing of Manoa, Dalila, and Harapha on Samson's final determination to destroy the Philistines constitutes the middle of the plot.[10] Although this question has been debated repeatedly since the time of Johnson and Cumberland, surprisingly little has been added to their opening words. The affirmative and the negative have attracted critics pretty equally; but since they have all been content to rely upon their own readings of the poem itself, apart from seventeenth-century conceptions of Greek tragedy, of Aristotle, or of the Samson story, their arguments, though often ingenious, have been inconclusive.[11]

The critical question of the dramatic quality of *Samson Agonistes* inevitably led students of Milton to inquire into the relationship between his tragedy and the tragic drama of the Greeks. Most of Milton's critics since Cumberland[12] have

---

[10] Cumberland's essay is reprinted in Todd, v, 333ff.

[11] Wordsworth—if his conversation was accurately reported—agreed with Johnson; see the diary of Crabbe Robinson, 7 January 1836, in Edith Morley, ed., *Henry Crabbe Robinson on Books and their Writers* (London, 1938), II, 479. For later critical discussions of this question, see the following: Max Beerbohm, "*Samson Agonistes* and *Zaza*," *Saturday Review of Literature*, LXXXIX (1900), 489; James W. Tupper, "The Dramatic Structure of *Samson Agonistes*," *PMLA*, XXXV (1920), 375-89; P. F. Baum, "*Samson Agonistes* Again," *PMLA*, XXXVI (1921), 354-71; E. C. Knowlton, "Causality in *Samson Agonistes*," *MLN*, XXXVII (1922), 333-39; W. C. Curry, "*Samson Agonistes* Yet Again," *Sewanee Review*, XXXII (1924), 336-52; and Emile Legouis, *A History of English Literature: the Middle Ages and the Renaissance*, rev. ed. (New York, 1935), p. 608f. The most recent comment on the dramatic structure of *Samson Agonistes* may be found in Una Ellis-Fermor's *The Frontiers of Drama* (London, 1946), where it is suggested that the poem would not be considered an artistic failure if it were regarded as religious drama rather than as tragedy. Unfortunately for this suggestion, the fact remains that Milton himself regarded the poem as a tragedy.

[12] He called it "as complete an imitation of the Ancient Tragedy, as the distance of times and the difference of languages will admit of," and the early editors filled their footnotes with numerous parallels between Milton's poem and the plays of Aeschylus, Sophocles, and Euripides.

assumed, or at least implied, that Milton intended *Samson Agonistes* primarily as an imitation of Greek tragedy. This assumption—for which there is strong evidence in the play itself and in Milton's preface to it—underlay both Hurd's praise and Johnson's censure. The opinion attributed to Coleridge is typical of the readers who take this side of the question; he is said to have called it "the finest imitation of the ancient Greek drama that ever had been, or ever would be written."[13] Sir Richard Jebb was the first to question this assumption. In an address delivered before the British Academy he denied that there is anything truly Greek about *Samson Agonistes*: he emphasized the strong Hebraic coloring of the poem, brought all the weight of his knowledge of the literature of the Greeks to support his opinion.[14] It was Jebb's address which stimulated the work of Professor W. R. Parker, who answered first with a paper in which he argued that *Samson Agonistes* is truly Greek in spirit because it is imbued with the "tone" of Greek tragedy. Professor Parker here defined this Hellenic "tone" as consisting in seriousness, thoughtfulness, didacticism, religiousness, and sublimity.[15] He must have realized readily, what is obvious to any reader of both literatures, that these features are equally as characteristic of much of the Old Testament as of Athenian tragedy, for he followed this paper a few years later with his much more substantial study, *Milton's Debt to Greek Tragedy in "Samson Agonistes."* His conclusion in this book was that, although Milton was especially indebted to the *Oedipus Coloneus* of Sophocles, *Samson Agonistes* is more than just an imitation of

---

[13] J. Payne Collier, ed., *Seven Lectures on Shakespeare and Milton* (London, 1856), p. xxvii. See also Masson, ed., *Works*, II, 584: "*Samson Agonistes* . . . was offered to the world as a tragedy avowedly of a different order from that which had been established in England. It was a tragedy of the severe classic order, according to that noble Greek model which had been kept up by none of the modern nations, unless it might be the Italians. In reading it, not Shakespeare, nor Ben Jonson, nor Massinger must be thought of, but Aeschylus, Sophocles, and Euripides."

[14] "*Samson Agonistes* and the Hellenic Drama," *Proceedings of the British Academy*, III (1907-1908), 341-48.

[15] "The Greek Spirit in Milton's *Samson Agonistes*," *Essays and Studies by Members of the English Association*, XX (1934), 21-44.

Greek tragedy; it is, rather—because Milton himself tapped the very roots of Sophocles' own inspiration—genuinely and originally Greek in its own right, an individual and independent work of art despite all debts.[16] The more one ponders Professor Parker's conclusion, the more one is convinced that the modification of his earlier opinion is more than verbal. His later statement seems to be an admission that *Samson Agonistes* cannot in any sense be accounted for or even understood by reference to Greek tragedy alone. His study leads one to marvel all the more at Milton's creative power as an English poet and makes Milton's achievement as a student of Greek tragedy seem relatively unimportant. But it is possible that the whole question of Milton's indebtedness to Greek tragedy can be settled only when someone has carefully studied the Greek plays in the forms in which Milton and his age knew them. Professor Parker read Greek tragedy in twentieth-century renderings; Milton did not. No one has yet studied the commentaries in Renaissance editions of Aeschylus, Sophocles, and Euripides to find what interpretation of their plays Milton was accustomed to.[17] Until this has been attempted, the entire dispute must remain unsettled and our generally accepted conception of the relationship of *Samson Agonistes* to Greek tragedy must be regarded as tentative.[18]

[16] (Baltimore, 1937), p. 249f.

[17] Davis P. Harding, *Milton and the Renaissance Ovid* (*Illinois Studies in Language and Literature*, XXX: Urbana, 1946), gives us a clear hint of what one might find if one made a study of Renaissance editions of Greek tragedy similar to his most informative investigation of Renaissance editions of Ovid. The heavy admixture of Christian attitudes and the application of the methods of biblical exegesis developed throughout the Middle Ages (e.g., allegorical, tropological, and anagogical interpretations) made *Ovidius Christianus* a figure totally different from *Ovidius Romanus*. Thus far we know nothing of *Sophocles Christianus*. Another case in point is the effect of the labors of Marsiglio Ficino upon the Renaissance interpretation of Plato.

[18] For additional discussion of the relation between *Samson Agonistes* and Greek drama, see Wilmon Brewer, "Two Athenian Models for *Samson Agonistes*," *PMLA*, XLII (1927), 910-20; and W. R. Parker, "The Kommos of Milton's *Samson Agonistes*," *SP*, XXXII (1935), 240-44. Gretchen L. Finney, "Chorus in *Samson Agonistes*," *PMLA*, LVIII (1943), 649-64, gives an interesting explanation of some of the peculiarities of Milton's use of chorus on the basis of Italian Renaissance drama.

The disagreement between Jebb and Mr. Parker might, perhaps, have arisen out of what one of Milton's critics has called the "counterpoint" of *Samson Agonistes*, a balancing of the Hebraism of content against the Hellenism of form.[19] Yet it is even more likely, I think, that the divergence of their opinions resulted from the overlapping of two periods of Miltonic criticism. The earlier, in which Jebb felt at home, was a period in which Milton was thought of as having been an awesome, grim, stern English poet, preeminently Christian and puritan. The clash between Jebb and Mr. Parker was a clash between an older representative of that period and a younger representative of the period which succeeded it, a period during which a "revaluation" took place, or was attempted. Since Jebb's day, there has been a tendency to see less Hebraism and more Hellenism in Milton's works as a whole; and Mr. Parker's insistence on Greek affinities in *Samson Agonistes* is a part of that larger critical movement which has spent itself only within the last few years, a movement which was a natural and desirable reaction against the older notion that Milton was an austerely puritan poet and a forbidding and unamiable man. But there has always been the danger of allowing this reaction to carry us too far, so that until recently we have made more and more of Milton's relations with the Renaissance at the risk of forgetting his place in the Reformation.[20] There is no doubt about the part which the exuberant paganism of the Italian Renaissance played in Milton's early works—especially, if not exclusively, in his Latin and Italian poems—but, on the other hand, in the later poems, and especially in *Samson Agonistes*, the

[19] F. Campbell Gray, "Milton's Counterpoint," *Sewanee Review*, XLIII (1935), 143. A similar view had been expressed earlier by E. N. S. Thompson, *Essays on Milton* (New Haven, 1914), p. 148.

[20] Lily B. Campbell, "The Christian Muse," *Huntington Library Bulletin*, October 1935, p. 70, has reminded us that Milton was in effect part of a movement which opposed the paganizing and secularizing of literature. The varied studies of such scholars as Fletcher, Willey, Lewis, Farnham, and Bush have, of late years, apprised us increasingly of the predominance of Christian over pagan elements and of the many essential survivals of medievalism in the culture of the Renaissance.

force of Hebraism is strong enough to be regarded as dominant.[21] It grows out of the very subject of *Samson Agonistes*: surely no passage of the Old Testament—with the possible exception of the Book of Esther—is more fraught with the hard vindictiveness of ancient Hebraism than the chapters of the Book of Judges which recount the story of Samson.

Ever since the time of Warburton, Milton's readers have been puzzled by this choice of subject.[22] How, they have repeatedly asked, did the author of epics about the Fall of Man and the Temptation of Christ happen to close his career with a poem about this brawling tribesman of Dan? Most critics have accepted, if only tacitly, the view of Masson, who thought that, although Milton's notes on subjects for tragedy in the Trinity Manuscript reveal that he had thought of Samson as a tragic hero long before he himself sat in darkness among Philistines, it was only the events of later years which brought to his mind the full force of that theme.[23] Pursuing this suggestion of Masson's, the critics have usually stressed the obvious parallels between the blind Samson enslaved by Philistines and the blind Milton in the midst of Cavaliers. Only Professor Hanford has offered another explanation for Milton's choice of this subject for the tragedy; he has found an analogy between Samson's sin and Adam's.[24]

But all the critics have found that they could not get at Milton's reasons for writing a tragedy about Samson without concerning themselves with what that tragedy means. One's speculation about Milton's choice of subject is inseparable from one's opinion about the total meaning of the poem. And there has never been anything like unanimity among the critics when this question has been discussed. A majority, it is true, have regarded the poem as, in the main, an auto-

---

[21] Wordsworth said that when Milton wrote *Samson Agonistes* "his mind was Hebraized. Indeed, his genius fed on the writings of the Hebrew prophets" (Grosart, ed., *Prose Works* [London, 1876], III, 461).

[22] Todd, ed., *Works*, III, 197.

[23] *Poetical Works of John Milton*, II, 580-83.

[24] "*Samson Agonistes* and Milton in Old Age," *loc.cit.*, p. 172. See also Hanford, "The Temptation Motive in Milton," *SP*, XV (1918), 176-94, for the bases of this argument.

biographical document and have given such reasons for Milton's using the subject as are to be found in the parallels between Samson and Milton already mentioned.[25] But the large minority of critics who have taken *Samson Agonistes* to be a political allegory have found it possible to make use of the same parallels.[26] The few critics who have regarded the tragedy as in some sense a moral or religious complement to *Paradise Lost* and *Paradise Regained* have been seriously handicapped by the lack of external historical evidence which the present study attempts, in part, to supply. Until such evidence has been provided and interpreted, all these conflicting views must be thought of as speculative.

Now and then a critic has sought with caution for the meaning of *Samson Agonistes* in its characters, assuming with justice that the meaning of this poem, as of any dramatic work, must reside primarily in the *personae* who are there thrown into conflict and trial. Thus a good deal has been written about the agents of Milton's tragedy. Scholars have called attention to the fact that the Book of Judges affords very little characterization of the people in this ancient story. There Manoa is hardly more than mentioned as Samson's father; Dalila is described merely as "a woman in the valley of Sorek"; Harapha does not exist; and Samson seems, to a modern reader, to be depicted as a swaggering, if consecrated, folk hero.[27]

[25] Todd, ed., *Works*, v, 488; Newton, ed., *Works*, III, 235; Masson, *Life*, VI, 670-78; Moody, ed., *Works*, p. xxxii; Verity, ed., *Samson Agonistes*, p. lviif.; Masson, ed., *Works*, II, 581f.; Pattison, *Milton*, p. 14f.; Cory, "Spenser, the School of the Fletchers, and Milton," *Univ. of Calif. Publications in Modern Philology*, II (1912), 371ff.; Saurat, *Milton: Man and Thinker*, pp. 236-43; Belloc, *Milton*, p. 273f.; Grierson, *Milton and Wordsworth: Poets and Prophets*, pp. 136-40; Menzies, "Milton: the Last Poems," *Essays and Studies by Members of the English Association*, XXIV (1939), 82-85; Tillyard, *Milton*, pp. 332-36, 346.

[26] Verity, *op.cit.*, p. lxif.; Todd, *op.cit.*, v, 339f.; Newton, *op.cit.*, III, 213; Brooke, *Milton*, p. 159f.; Ramsay, "Morality Themes in Milton's Poetry," *SP*, XV (1918), 155-57; Clark, "Milton's Earlier Samson," *Texas Univ. Studies in English*, VII (1927), 149, 154; Belloc, *Milton*, p. 17.

[27] The best critical discussions of Manoa, Dalila, and Harapha may be found in Newton, *op.cit.*, III, 264; Perceval, *op.cit.*, pp. lv-lix; Parker, *Milton's Debt*, pp. 119ff.; Hughes, *op.cit.*, p. 433f.; and Daniel Boughner, "Milton's Harapha and Renaissance Comedy," *ELH*, XI (1944), 297-306,

And yet, all critics agree, Milton somehow brought these slender figures to life, endowed them with unforgettably distinct features of personality, and thrust them together in a clash of mind and spirit of the magnitude found only in the greatest poetry. This, it is generally agreed, is the miracle wrought by the poet, and it has its center in Samson himself. Every reader of the poem has marveled at the alchemy by means of which Milton transmuted this bare biblical character, whose story as told in Judges seems to a modern reader to be almost brutal in its violence, into a tragic hero of great spiritual stature. Perceval compared Milton's Samson favorably with Oedipus and Prometheus,[28] and other critics have praised the characterization enthusiastically. Professor E. M. Clark, who has contributed the most thorough analysis of Milton's portrait of Samson, has suggested that the poet heightened and transformed the biblical character by omitting some of his features, by emphasizing his comeliness, by amplifying his mentality, and by elevating him emotionally and morally, with the result that, as he appears in *Samson Agonistes*, he is beautified, strengthened spiritually, and greatly humanized.[29]

3

HERETOFORE no one has sought to discover whether this wonderful transmutation was entirely the product of the poet's own sense of the tragic—as nearly every critic has assumed—or whether Milton built upon a historical tradition which had already evolved a conception of Samson strikingly different from that afforded by the Book of Judges alone. This study

---

though Mr. Boughner seems to me to have pushed his evidence too far. See also *TLS*, 2 January 1937, p. 12; 16 January 1937, p. 44; and 23 January 1937, p. 60, for notes on the origin of Harapha and the etymology of his name.

[28] *Op.cit.*, pp. xxiff.

[29] "Milton's Conception of Samson," *Texas Univ. Studies in English*, VIII (1928), 88-99. Similar estimates of Samson may be found in Hanford, "*Samson Agonistes* and Milton in Old Age," *loc.cit.*, pp. 174-83; Verity, *op.cit.*, pp. liii-lv; Baum, *op.cit.*, p. 356f.; Grierson, "A Note upon the *Samson Agonistes* of John Milton," *loc.cit.*, pp. 3-7; Tillyard, *Milton*, p. 331; Parker, *Milton's Debt*, pp. 110-16; Whiting, *op.cit.*, p. 259f.

is directed, first of all, towards a solution of that problem, though that problem, as will be shown, leads us far beyond itself.

Professor Hughes is the only scholar who has ventured near it at all. He has noticed that in John Donne's *Biathanatos* (III, v, 4) Samson is referred to as a saint, and he remarks that Milton was probably familiar with this seventeenth-century conception of the Danite leader. Nevertheless Professor Hughes believes that Milton rejected this notion of Samson, that Milton turned from the accepted view of Samson as saint in order to make him a "genuinely tragic" hero.[30] There are, however, serious weaknesses in this argument. There is no explicit, indisputable evidence in the poem itself, although at one point in the play (lines 1268-96) the Chorus, singing at first joyfully of the glory beheld when God sends a "deliverer" to His people armed with "celestial vigour" and invincible strength "to quell the mighty," suddenly changes its mood and confronts the hard reality of its champion's predicament:

> But patience is more oft the exercise
> Of Saints, the trial of thir fortitude,
> Making them each his own Deliverer,
> And Victor over all
> That tyrannie or fortune can inflict.

As the Chorus continues, addressing Samson directly, it is made plain that at least Samson's fellows expect saintliness of him. They remind him that he was "with might endu'd Above the Sons of men," and that for this reason the glorious actions of a divinely appointed deliverer may yet be his. Then they remember his blindness, his dejection, and they conclude,

> But sight bereav'd
> May chance to number thee with those
> Whom Patience finally must crown.

Are we free to read these lines without the context of the previous statement that saints are most often distinguished

by patience? If not, then we must grant that the Chorus—
and perhaps Milton as well—accepted Samson as a saint.
There is no explicit denial of his sainthood in the poem, and
in the end he suffers martyrdom in such a way as to conform
exactly to the Chorus's description here of saintly deportment.

There is more to be said under this head, but it must be re-
served until more reliable external evidence has been presented. Without that evidence, one can argue that Milton's
Samson is a saint only on the basis of a possibly subjective
reading of the poem itself and on a more general opinion that
the view of Professor Hughes makes Milton too much like
us of the twentieth century. We usually assume that a saint is
not a suitable tragic hero. Did Milton work from the same
assumption? Before answering such a question one must remind himself of Milton's place in time and of his relation to
his own period. We must not forget the profoundly religious
cast of Milton's mind nor forget the extent to which, in an
age strongly tinctured with medievalism, his personal outlook
was medieval. He was, indeed, what his most provocative, if
most often mistaken, critic has called him: "le porte-parole
d'une tradition antique et complexe."[31]

It is that ancient and complex tradition behind *Samson
Agonistes*, the ideological context of the poem, with which
this book is concerned. My purpose is to provide the twentieth-century reader with a knowledge of that part of the
Christian tradition which has been ignored hitherto by critics
of *Samson Agonistes* but which is indispensable to a true
reading of that tragedy.

The questions underlying this study are these: what were

[31] Of course, Saurat ("La Cabale et la Philosophie de Milton," *Revue des
Etudes Juives*, LXXIII [1921], 13) was thinking of the Cabala when he
used this phrase, and I am not.

The best-balanced statement of Milton's affinities with medieval view-
points is that by Douglas Bush: *The Renaissance and English Humanism*
(Toronto, 1939), ch. IV. Kester Svendsen, "Milton and the Encyclopedias
of Science," *SP*, XXXIX (1942), 326f., has shown that even Milton's sci-
entific lore was somewhat out of date, drawn, as it seems to have been,
from encyclopedias of science which were thoroughly medieval in com-
plexion, and which contained little or no information derived from the
embryonic new science of the seventeenth century.

the implicit assumptions made about Samson and his story by Milton and his readers? what, in other words, was the shape of the seventeenth-century conception of Samson? An attempt is here made to answer these questions by tracing the history of the Samson-idea from the Old Testament to *Samson Agonistes.*

Most of this history and most of the tradition revealed by it are to be found in the hermeneutic and homiletic literature of Christianity.[32] From the biblical commentaries, the sermons, the *exempla*, and other writings of the Fathers of the early Church, the Schoolmen of the late Middle Ages, and the learned divines of the Renaissance, we can descry and reconstruct the Samson tradition which lies behind, and between the lines of, Milton's tragedy, the attitude towards the hero which Milton expected his "fit audience" to have.[33]

---

[32] As I remarked in the preface, this approach to the poem was first suggested by Allan H. Gilbert, *MLN*, XLI (1926), 266f. Jonathan Richardson seems to have been the first critic of Milton who cited a patristic source: *Explanatory Notes and Remarks on Milton's "Paradise Lost"* (London, 1734), p. 521. More recently A. O. Lovejoy sought the sources of part of Milton's theology in the literature of medieval Christianity ("Milton and the Paradox of the Fortunate Fall," *ELH*, IV [1937], 169). In 1761 Newton referred to "the best commentators" on the Bible for elucidation of a passage in *Samson Agonistes* (*op.cit.*, III, 234). Todd reviewed the Schoolmen's opinion of Samson as a suicide (*op.cit.*, V, 476), and Grierson has cited Augustine in the same connection ("A Note upon the *Samson Agonistes* of John Milton," *loc.cit.*, p. 2f.).

[33] Some work of this sort has already been done with the other major poems of Milton. Elizabeth Marie Pope's excellent study, *"Paradise Regained": the Tradition and the Poem* (Baltimore, 1947), has revealed the complex relationship between that poem and the traditional conceptions of the Temptation of Christ; and the extent to which her findings and those presented here are in agreement is suggested below, pp. 125ff. Attempts have been made to elucidate specific details of *Paradise Lost* in the light of hexameral and hermeneutic literature: Grant McColley, "Milton's Battle in Heaven and Rupert of St. Heribert," *Speculum*, XVI (1941), 230-35; and "Milton's Ariel," *N&Q*, CLXXVI, 45; Arnold Williams, "Milton and the Renaissance Commentaries on Genesis," *MP*, XXXVII (1939-1940), 264-67, and "Renaissance Commentaries on Genesis and Some Elements of the Theology of *Paradise Lost*," *PMLA*, LVI (1941), 151-64; Allan H. Gilbert, "The Theological Basis of Satan's Rebellion and the Function of Abdiel" in *Paradise Lost*," *MP*, XL (1942-1943), 24-27; Sister Mary Irma Corcoran, *Milton's Paradise with Reference to the Hexaemeral Background* (Catholic Univ. of America dissertation, 1945); Martin A. Larson, *The Modernity of Milton: a Theological and Philosophical Investigation* (Chicago, 1927).

It is well known that Milton was learned in these writings. There are numerous citations of the Church Fathers and their successors in his prose works, and on many occasions in both prose and verse he adopted the thinking of these writers, or at least confronted and considered their opinions before diverging from them.[34] Milton was equipped to read the Bible in Latin, in Greek, in Hebrew, including the Targumim, or Aramaic paraphrases of the Old Testament, and the Syriac version of the New Testament; and he was also conversant with all the intricate problems of exegesis dealt with by the textual criticism of his day. Indeed, as Professor Fletcher has said, "virtually all of the scholarly apparatus of the biblical student of his day was at his command."[35]

Milton believed that a knowledge of the literature of biblical exegesis was a necessary part of the learning of an educated man. In his *Tract of Prelatical Episcopacy* (1641), he expressed what appears to be a considered opinion of the value of knowing the patristic literature:

He that thinks it the part of a well-learned man, to have read diligently the ancient stories of the Church, and to be no stranger in the volumes of the Fathers shall have all judicious men consenting with him; not hereby to controule, and new fangle the

[34] The most satisfying general discussion of Milton's knowledge of, use of, and attitude towards the Fathers is John P. Pritchard's article, "The Fathers of the Church in the Works of John Milton," *Classical Journal*, XXXIII (1937-1938), 79-84. Kathleen Hartwell, *Lactantius and Milton* (Cambridge, Mass., 1929) reveals the dangers waiting upon a study restricted to only one of the many patristic writers whom Milton knew. Among the numerous commentators cited, quoted, or mentioned by Milton are these: Philo Judaeus, Diodorus Siculus, Irenaeus, Clement of Alexandria, Origen, Cyprian, Lactantius, Athanasius, Basil, Procopius, Sulpicius Severus, Ambrose, Chrysostom, Jerome, Augustine, Theodoret, Prudentius, Gregory the Great, Isidore of Seville, Erasmus, Luther, Calvin, Grotius, Buxtorf, Pareus, Capell, Bucer, John Diodati, and Henry Bullinger. The Commonplace Book alone reveals an amazingly scholarly knowledge of hermeneutics, as was shown by Hanford, "The Chronology of Milton's Private Studies," *PMLA*, XXXVI (1921), 313f.

[35] "Milton's Use of Biblical Quotations," *JEGP*, XXVI (1927), 149, 165. Professor Fletcher pursued his inquiry further in his *The Use of the Bible in Milton's Prose* (*Univ. of Illinois Studies in Language and Literature*, XIV [1929], 289-464). See also Barker, "Milton's Schoolmasters," *MLR*, XXXII (1937), 518f., where it is shown that Milton's teacher, Thomas Young, was also deeply read in the writings of the Fathers.

Scripture, *God* forbid, but to marke how corruption . . . crept in by degrees, and to gather up . . . the remaining sparks of Originall truth, . . . weighing the Fathers in the ballance of Scripture.[36]

He would have his readers "take the good which wee light on in the Fathers, and set it to oppose the evill which other men seek from them." As far as we can tell, this was Milton's attitude throughout his life. The Scriptures were his highest authority, but he knew the Fathers, used them whenever they helped him understand the meaning of Scripture, and opposed violently any misuse of them. Even at the end of his career, in the defense of tragedy prefixed to *Samson Agonistes*, he recalled, and appealed to, the example of Gregory Nazianzen, who "thought it not unbecoming the sanctity of his person to write a Tragedy, which he entitl'd *Christ Suffering*."

Because Milton himself was deeply learned in the entire literature of Christian hermeneutics, and because he assumed that an educated reader would "be no stranger in the volumes of the Fathers," we are not only justified in seeking but compelled to seek whatever aid those writings may afford when we try to understand Milton's treatment of a figure whom those writings helped to shape in the Christian mind of the seventeenth century.

Milton's age, like every other, had its roots deep in the past. Milton's bonds with that past were especially strong because he was a learned man at a time when learning consisted almost entirely in knowledge of the past. It is for this reason that his writings demanded of his audience, and still demand, learning nearly commensurate with his own. For Milton's contemporary readers, there was comparatively little danger of misreading *Samson Agonistes*; in their minds the conception of Samson evolved by the first seventeen centuries of the Christian tradition was still clear and intact. But that conception of Samson began to fade and dissolve before the end of the seventeenth century. Today it is not only lost; it is completely forgotten. It is time for us—unless we are content

[36] Columbia edition, III, 101.

to misconstrue *Samson Agonistes*—to attempt to reacquire that forgotten conception.

This book is not in any sense a source-study nor an inquiry into indebtednesses. Throughout the next four chapters the reader is asked to follow a reconstruction of the tradition which grew up about the biblical account of Samson during the first seventeen centuries of the Christian era. Although there is rather little development in this tradition in some periods, it is necessary to present a generous selection from it at several chronological stages in order to give the reader a full sense of its vastness and its weight. In the final chapter I attempt to suggest what effect this reconstructed tradition has upon our reading of *Samson Agonistes*. But a word of warning must be given: the effect of this presentation is mainly cumulative. The reader who returns to Milton's tragedy with the general outlines of this tradition in mind should find the poem enriched with new levels of old meaning. He will not find that this study, nor any other, fully explains *Samson Agonistes*. Such an inquiry as this, even if it wanders far and seems at times to deal with writers of slight or no fame, can cut only a narrow and shadowy trail through the wilderness of the history of man's mind.

Still one more preliminary word. Since this study is not meant to prove that Milton was "indebted" to any one writer or to any group of writers, and since nearly everything ever written about Samson was compounded, absorbed, and repeated by each new commentator, we cannot confine our attention only to writings which Milton knew, or even to those writings which were available to him and his contemporaries. As it happens, nearly all the writers who contributed to this tradition were known to studious men in Milton's time. Most of the hermeneutic literature on which this study rests was in print in the fifteenth, sixteenth, and seventeenth centuries —if only, as is true of some parts of it, in the quotations which appeared in marginal and interlinear glosses in various editions of the Bible and in the more extended biblical commentaries and historical works of the Renaissance and Reformation. Even those of Milton's audience who were not personally familiar with these scholarly works of exegesis were subject to their influence when they sat under their preachers or read the popular literature of the day.

Chapter II

THE FOUNDATIONS OF THE
SAMSON TRADITION

THE earliest known version of the story of Samson is contained in the thirteenth, fourteenth, fifteenth, and sixteenth chapters of the Book of Judges. Since these four chapters of the Old Testament are the basis of the tradition with which we are here concerned, it is necessary to pause long enough to inquire into their origin and examine their contents with some care.

1

MOST, if not all, of the Book of Judges is now thought to be comprised of traditional material which may have been transmitted orally for several centuries before it was written down.[1] Of all the contents of this book of the Old Testament, the Samson story most clearly reveals its origin in popular poetic sagas or triumphal poems. Indeed, Professor Albright has referred to it as "nearly pure folklore."[2] Frazer found and described numerous analogues of the Samson story in the oral and written folklore of widely separated cultures,[3] and Ginzberg has brought to light much evidence which shows that the elements of the story are scattered throughout He-

[1] Cf. William F. Albright, *From the Stone Age to Christianity: Monotheism and the Historical Process* (Baltimore, 1940), ch. v, on which most of the first section of this chapter is based. See also George F. Moore, *A Critical and Exegetical Commentary on Judges* (New York, 1895), pp. xix-xxix, xxxiii-xxxviii, 312-15; L. E. P. Erith, "Judges," in *A New Commentary on Holy Scripture,* ed. C. Gore, H. L. Goudge, and A. Guillaume (New York, 1929), pp. 198-200; J. R. Dummelow, ed., *A Commentary on the Holy Bible by Various Writers* (New York, 1938), pp. 155-58; R. L. Ottley, *Aspects of the Old Testament* (London and New York, 1897), p. 147; J. R. Peters, *The Religion of the Hebrews* (Cambridge, Mass., 1923), p. 186; Samuel R. Driver, *An Introduction to the Literature of the Old Testament* (New York, 1891), p. 154f.

[2] P. 209.

[3] *Folk-lore in the Old Testament: Studies in Comparative Religion, Legend, and Law* (London, 1919), *passim.* Cf. Moore, *op.cit.,* p. 364f.

braic legend.[4] The oral story is at least as old as the first quarter of the twelfth century B.C., when, after a long struggle against the Canaanites, during which they gained national unity, the Hebrews were set upon by even more vigorous and dangerous enemies, the Philistines and the Tsikal, who came "from the regions of the Aegean, bringing a rude barbaric energy from the north as well as exotic culture of Mycenean type."[5] The raw materials of which the story was compounded are certainly more ancient still.

Even before the Philistine invasion, which provides the setting of the Samson story in its written form, the tribes of Israel had developed a vague system of political leadership which consisted in reliance on heads of clans (like Othniel), warriors (like Barac or Gideon), men of wealth (like Jair), adventurers (like Jephthah), priests (like Eli), and prophets (like Samuel). Inevitably, legendary or semilegendary figures were fitted by later narrators into a setting which gave them an appearance of historicity. The leaders of the several types mentioned above were given the rather general designation of *shophet*, usually translated "judge." Albright explains that these tribal leaders were at first just "local personages [who] became distinguished far and wide for their wisdom," so that "men came to them from increasing distances for adjudication of disputes." But because mere human wisdom was not sufficient qualification for a judge, "his fame for wisdom and honesty was supplemented by a reputation as a special agent of divine power." Thus the power of divination was attributed to Samuel. And when the heroic legend of Samson was adapted to later uses and placed beside the record of more purely historical judges, he, too, long credited with unusual strength, was said to wield a superhuman strength which was the special gift of God; and he was also depicted as a leader especially consecrated from birth as a Nazarite, which meant

---

[4] *The Legends of the Jews*, trans. Henrietta Szold (Philadelphia, 1910-1938), *passim*.

[5] Albright, p. 218f.

that he was dedicated by prescribed rites to a life of austere asceticism.[6]

The Samson pericope was probably written down as early as the tenth century B.C.[7] In the latter part of the seventh century, classical Hebrew literature was greatly altered by the Deuteronomic reforms, a reactionary movement which sought to revive the Mosaic spirit in Judaism. Along with a revival of emphasis on monotheism in this period went a strengthened concept of divine justice. It was in this period and under the influence of this movement that the narratives now found in the Book of Judges were gathered together and rigorously edited to unify the several stories and to lay stress on the theme of divine punishment for national sin. By virtue of the addition of most of Judges 13, and of a number of minor interpolations in chapters 14, 15, and 16, the Samson story was not only linked with the other stories of Israel's judges but was also elevated to the level of a religious document. Although the qualities of a good story were not effaced by such revision, there are obvious inconsistencies in the Samson chapters which probably result from these Deuteronomic alterations.[8]

Thus the story of Samson, as we read it today in the Book of Judges, represents in itself an ancient and massive tradition and a long process of development from oral folklore, through written folklore containing historical matter, to sacred Scripture instinct with much of the religious life of the ancient Jews.

2

IN THIS account we are told that at a time when God punished the children of Israel for their evil-doing by giving them into bondage to the Philistines for forty years, an angel appeared to the wife of Manoa, a Danite of Zora. This woman was barren, but the angel told her that she would conceive and give birth to a son, and he admonished her to refrain from strong drink and unclean food. He also told her that her

[6] Albright, p. 216f.   [7] Albright, p. 209.   [8] Albright, p. 244f.

son would be a Nazarite, consecrated to God from the womb, that his locks should not be shorn, and that he would begin the liberation of Israel. When the woman told her husband of the angel's coming, of his awesome countenance, and of his instructions regarding the son whose birth he foretold, Manoa himself prayed to God that the angel might be sent again to instruct them further. God answered Manoa's prayer by sending the angel a second time to the woman when her husband was not with her. But she ran to Manoa and brought him before the angel. Manoa then asked the angel whether it was he who had appeared before to the woman, and, when the angel said that it had been he, Manoa begged him to tell them again of the care they were to take of their promised son. When the angel had repeated what he had said before to the wife, Manoa implored the angel to wait while they prepared food for him. This the angel refused, commanding them instead to make an offering to God. Nor would the angel tell Manoa his name, which, he explained, was a secret. When, therefore, Manoa had lighted the sacrificial fire, the angel ascended towards heaven in the flames; and Manoa and his wife fell down in fear and wonder. The angel came no more to them, but Manoa knew that it had come from the Lord, and he told his wife that he feared that they would die, for surely they had looked upon the face of God. But she was confident that God would not have accepted their offering, nor revealed to them such wonders, nor promised them a son if He had meant to destroy them.

In time Manoa's wife bore a son, whom she called Samson. As the boy grew in the camp of Dan, the Holy Spirit worked within him. Once when he was in Timnath, Samson was pleased by the sight of a woman whom he saw there. When he returned to his home he told his mother and father that he wanted the woman for his wife. Although they objected to his marrying a Philistine, he insisted, saying only that she pleased him. He did not tell them, and they did not know, that this was God's will and that Samson was seeking an occasion for making war against the Philistines, who were then the masters of his people. But his father and mother yielded to his demand and went to Timnath. And Samson, too, went again to Timnath. As he was nearing the vineyards of that place a young lion rushed upon him roaring. Samson pulled the beast to pieces with his hands and went on to join his parents without telling them what he had done. After Samson had been to Timnath he returned to the place where he had slain the lion. There he found a honeycomb in the carcass and bees swarming in it. He carried honey in his hands to his father and mother without telling them where he had got it. When the marriage agreement had been made, Samson held a feast. The bride's tribe appointed thirty men to accompany the bridegroom. To these companions Samson proposed a riddle, promising them that if they were able to solve it within seven days he would give them gifts of clothing. The riddle was: "Out of the eater came forth meat, sweetness out of the strong one." But when they had sought in vain to solve the riddle, they approached Samson's bride, threatening to burn her and her family if she did not learn the answer from Samson and tell it to them. For this reason Samson's bride begged him tearfully to tell her the meaning of the riddle. Finally he yielded to her pleading, and she in turn revealed the answer to his retainers. On the seventh day they gave Samson the answer: "What is sweeter than honey? and what is stronger than a lion?" Samson was enraged and knew that they had learned it from his bride. Then he went to Askalon, slew thirty men there, and brought back their garments, which he distributed among his thirty retainers. Afterwards he returned in wrath to his father's house.

While he was away Samson's bride was given in marriage to one of the companions whom Samson had used as his friend. When Samson returned to his bride with a gift, he was turned away from the house by her father, who told him that he thought Samson hated her and that he had, for that reason, given her to another. Samson declared then that the Philistines would never get anything but enmity from him thereafter. And straightway he caught three hundred foxes, tied them tail to tail with firebrands between them, lighted the brands, and drove the foxes into the fields of the Philistines, where all their crops stood ready for harvest. When they learned that Samson had done this, the Philistines burnt the woman of Timnath and her father. Samson was resolved never to cease harassing the Philistines until he had avenged himself. In a great battle which followed, he inflicted heavy losses on his enemies.

After this battle Samson withdrew to the summit of the rock of Etam. Meanwhile the Philistines advanced into Juda and pitched camp in Lehi. The Jews were fearful and asked the Philistines why they menaced them with arms, and the Philistines told them that they were seeking Samson. It was then that Samson's own people went up to him and asked him to surrender to the Philistines, lest they make an entire nation suffer for his deeds. When the Jews guaranteed him safe conduct to the camp of the Philistines, Samson yielded and went with them in bonds to the camp in Lehi. But when Samson was brought, bound, before the Philistines, they jeered at him. The Lord strengthened Samson then so that he was able to break his bonds. Smiting the Philistines with the jawbone of an ass, he killed that day a thousand men. Afterwards he boasted of the feat and threw down the jawbone, naming the place Ramath-Lehi. But Samson was thirsty. When he called upon God to quench his thirst, acknowledging that he had done great deeds for his people only with God's aid, a fountain gushed forth from the jawbone, and he named the place En-hakkore. Thereafter he was a judge in Israel for twenty years.

At another time Samson went to Gaza and consorted with a harlot there. When the Philistines heard that he was in the city they set guards at the gates to lie in wait for him, planning to capture him and kill him when he tried to go out in the morning. But Samson rose at midnight and went out of Gaza carrying the gates of the city away with him to the top of a hill near Hebron.

Afterwards Samson loved a woman of Sorek named Dalila,

to whom the satraps of the Philistines came promising a reward of eleven hundred pieces of silver if she would learn from Samson the secret of his strength and reveal it to them. Dalila cajoled, flattered, and importuned Samson to tell her the secret of his strength, and how he could be made weak. Three times she tried him; three times he answered her evasively; three times she called the satraps to take him prisoner; three times he easily broke the bonds she bound him with. But finally he yielded to her blandishments and told her that he was a Nazarite consecrated to God from the very womb of his mother, and that he would be as weak as any other man if his locks were shorn. Then Dalila, having called the Philistines, made Samson sleep in her lap, and while he slept there they cut off his hair. When he awoke he thought he would shake off his bonds as he had done before, but he found himself powerless and at the mercy of his enemies. The Philistines blinded him and took him as a captive to Gaza, where they fettered him and forced him to work at a mill.

Subsequently, during his captivity, his hair grew again. And then one day the Philistines summoned him from his prison to make sport for them while they celebrated a festival in honor of their god Dagon. During a pause in the events of the festival, Samson was made to stand between two great pillars which supported the roof of the building wherein all the Philistines of rank were seated. It was then that Samson asked the boy who led him to allow him to touch the columns with either hand that he might lean upon them to rest. When he had grasped the columns with either hand, Samson pushed against them with all his strength, calling upon God to aid him in avenging himself against those who had blinded him and crying, "Let me die with the Philistines!" The temple fell down upon the thousands who were within it, and Samson, too, was killed, so that he slew more in dying than he had during all the rest of his life.

He was buried by his kinsmen in the burying-ground of his family between Zora and Eshtaol.

3

THIS is the whole of the strange story of Samson as it is told in the Book of Judges. Like its more artistic counterpart, the Book of Esther, the Samson story is a very ancient example of intensely nationalistic literature. The form in which it was left by the Deuteronomic editor, in fact, heightens the nationalistic character of this old folk story, which was redacted to teach how evils befell the children of Israel when they sinned and "went a-whoring after other gods" (Judges 2:17). For Jehovah was, from the Judaic point of view, the God of a people, a Chosen People, and faithfulness to their jealous racial deity could be most clearly proved by rendering great service—in that era usually great military or political service —to the nation which acknowledged Him as Creator. It is difficult for one in the twentieth century to understand how this tribal hero became an important figure in later Christian literature.

If this had been the only mention of Samson in the Bible, his career might not have been given much attention during the Christian era. But Samson was also mentioned in the Epistle to the Hebrews, which was attributed, throughout the period with which we are here concerned, to Saint Paul. In this letter Samson is referred to as an example of those who were victorious through faith in a list which includes Abel, Enoch, Noah, Abraham, Sarah, Isaac, Jacob, Joseph, Moses, and Rahab, and which ends in this way:

What shall I more say? for time would fail me to tell of Gedeon, and of Barac, and of Samson, and of Jephtha; and of David also, and Samuel, and of the prophets: who through faith subdued kingdoms, wrought righteousness, obtained promises, stopped the mouths of lions, quenched the violence of fire, escaped the edge of the sword, out of weakness were made strong, waxed valiant in fight, turned to flight the armies of aliens.[9]

The place given to Samson in this august company of all the great of the Old Testament by a writer of no less authority

[9] Hebrews 11:32-34 (Authorized Version).

than Saint Paul marks a divergence, at the very beginning of the Christian era, between the Hebraic and the Christian conceptions of Samson. The author of this sermon in epistolary form, addressed to Christianized Jews, wrote with the purpose of reminding them that Judaism had been superseded by a higher form of religion, in which everything that had gone before was caught up, absorbed, and transmuted. Here, according to the Pauline doctrine of the election of true believers, Samson was set down as one of the chosen (*electi*) of the Old Testament. Later Christian writers made *electus* synonymous with *sanctus* in this connection and accepted such Old Testament personages as saints in a rather special sense. Thus the ground was defined on which Samson could be adopted by Christianity, and the bond between the world of the Old Testament and the world of the New was strengthened from the first by an apostolic writer. But the disparity between the Samson of Judges and the Samson of Hebrews placed before Christian exegetes a problem which in later periods was to cause them great difficulty.

Chapter III

THE SAMSON OF THE PATRISTIC PERIOD

URING the first seven centuries of the Christian
era a mass of hermeneutic literature grew up
around the four chapters of the Book of Judges,
which chronicled the career of this religio-political
hero of Judaism, and the two verses of the Epistle to the
Hebrews, which anticipated the terms of this hero's acceptance by Christianity as an exemplar of faith. This hermeneutic
literature is various and complex, but it can be described by
defining with illustrative examples the several main directions
in which it developed. There was the *literal* interpretation of
the Samson story, descending from the Antiochan school of
historio-grammatical exegesis, which sometimes took the form
of mere retelling without explicit interpretation, which included the rhetorical use of Samson in arguments in favor of
chastity, and which resulted in the conception of Samson as
saint, necessitating an explanation of his fall and redemption.
There was also, concomitant with literal interpretation and
often threatening to displace it, the *allegorical* interpretation
of Samson, descending from the Alexandrian school of exegesis,[1] which elevated Samson still higher in the Christian
mind by making him a figure of Christ. These were the two
main currents of the Samson tradition in the Middle Ages.
But there was also a third element which, although not a
major part of the direct patristic tradition, antedated it and
survived throughout the first seventeen centuries of the Christian era. This was the equation of Samson with Hercules,
which will be discussed at the end of the present chapter.

---

[1] See the excellent essay by Wilhelm Dilthey, "Die Entstehung der Hermeneutik," in *Die Geistige Welt: Einleitung in die Philosophie des Lebens*,
I (*Gesammelte Schriften*, ed. Georg Misch [Leipzig and Berlin, 1924], v,
317-38, esp. 322f.).

1

IN 277 B.C. the biblical account of the life of Samson was made
accessible to the Greek world in the Septuagint version of
the Old Testament, but it was not until three centuries later
that the extra-biblical Samson tradition commenced. The early
rabbinical exegetes—Ezra, Hillel, and Philo—were concerned
principally with the Pentateuch and its theological problems.
The later books of the Old Testament were not thoroughly
interpreted until the first century of the Christian era, when
the Jews attempted to present the whole of their culture and
their history to the world of Gentiles. It was in this period
that Flavius Josephus wrote his monumental *Jewish Antiquities*, a full history of the Jews from the time of the Creation,
based on the Old Testament. Although there is no evidence
to indicate that his handling of the Samson story was influential until after the appearance of the *Historia Scholastica* of
Petrus Comestor in the twelfth century, it is properly the
opening of this inquiry because its interpretation of Samson
is essentially literal and because it was the earliest extra-biblical retelling in full of a story often retold in following centuries.[2]

Josephus' treatment of the story of Samson is very close
to the account in the Book of Judges; however—probably because he was consciously trying to present Jewish history in
the most reasonable and favorable light—he made additions
to the story which amount to interpretation. He supplied
what might be called poetic motivation for parts of the plot

[2] All quotations from Josephus are given in the words of the translation
by Thomas Lodge: *The Famous and Memorable Works of Josephus* (London, 1640), pp. 120-23. This translation is very close to the original. Cf.
Antiquities, v, x, in Henry St. John Thackeray, trans., *Josephus* ("Loeb
Classical Library"), v, 124-43. Josephus was often cited as an authority on
Samson from the twelfth century on, but especially in the sixteenth and
seventeenth centuries. The number of references to Josephus in such a standard seventeenth-century work as Matthew Poole's *Synopsis Criticorum*
(London, 1669) is an index of his importance to biblical exegesis in that
period. Lodge's translation was printed eight times between 1602 and
1640. For Milton's references to Josephus, cf. F. A. Patterson and F. R.
Fogle, *An Index to the Columbia Edition of the Works of John Milton*
(New York, 1940).

in which the original version did not have clear probability. Thus he made Manoa's wife "most famous for her beauty" in order to explain that Manoa prayed for the second appearance of the angel because "he loved his wife so exceedingly, that he almost doted on her, and for this occasion he was extremely jealous of her." Josephus also endeavored to make the story more attractive to a wide audience by heightening, ennobling, and even prettifying the setting and the characters. Manoa, who in the Book of Judges was designated simply as "a certain man of the tribe of Dan," becomes in Josephus' rendering "an excellent man, . . . one of the chiefest of the tribe of *Dan*, . . . the only esteemed Prince amongst them." According to Josephus, Samson was "endowed with an excellent beauty both of minde and body," was sober, and was possessed of "some propheticall and more then humane forwardnesse," and he says of him at last:

He was a man of great vertue, force and magnanimitie: and especially in that which concerneth his end, he meriteth to be admired at, because that even unto this latter hour he was animated against the Philistines. And whereas he was allured and besotted by a woman, it ought to be attributed to humane nature, which is so weak that it cannot resist sinne: otherwise in all other things, we ought to yeeld testimonie of his vertue.

Josephus did as much as could be done by Judaism, within the bounds of a strictly literal interpretation, to magnify, justify, and ennoble this rather unwieldy racial hero. If this much was possible solely on the basis of a literal interpretation of Judges 13-16, it is not surprising that Samson could be made completely acceptable to Christianity when his fame was enhanced by Hebrews 11:32-4 and by allegorical interpretation.

Among the Christian writers of the patristic period, those who merely repeated, summarized, or paraphrased the account of Samson in Judges as it appeared in the great Vulgate translation of Jerome were far less resourceful and original than Josephus;[3] but their repetition of the story, based on an un-

---

[3] See the prose summary of the Samson story in Sulpicius Severus, *Chroni-*

questioning faith in Holy Scripture and a complete acceptance of its literal sense, served to disseminate widely the knowledge of Samson's career. Similar are the accounts of Samson included in such annals of world history as the *Chronicon Paschale*, supposed to be the work of Idatius of Chaves (fifth century), and the *De Orte et Obitu Patrum* of Isidore of Seville (d. 636).[4] These historical writings are more explicitly literal than the mere repetitions of the story as religious *mythos*, because such annals perpetuated the Samson story as manifest history. One of the results of this historical acceptance of Samson was that important writers in this period and in later times referred to Samson more and more often as the ruler and liberator of Israel, a personage whose historicity was as unquestionable as Julius Caesar's.[5]

Perhaps the most interesting literal treatments of Samson were the homiletic ones. Even before the end of the first century, Clement of Rome used Samson as an *a fortiori* example in the argument for chastity,[6] and numerous writers and

ca, 1, 27f. (*Corp. Scrip. Eccles. Lat.* [Vienna, 1866], 1, 30f.). There are also paraphrases of the story in verse: e.g., Paulinus of Nola, *Poema XXIV*, lines 599-686 (*Pat. Lat.*, LXI, 626-28); and Cyprian, *Iudicum*, lines 482-720, in *Heptateuchos*, ed. R. Peiper (*Corp. Scrip. Eccles. Lat.* [Vienna, 1891], XXIII, 198-207). A collation of the LXX, the popular Junius-Tremellius Latin Bible of the Renaissance, and the Authorized Version does not reveal any differences which are material to the history of the interpretation of Samson. The LXX is "literary" in style, an extremely careful hypotactic rendering of the original Hebrew; the Vulgate is beautifully simple, plain, and paratactic; the Junius-Tremellius translation gives the impression of being a Latin adaptation of the style of the Septuagint, and, indeed, it is based on both the LXX and the Hebrew; the Authorized Version is stylistically reminiscent of the Vulgate.

[4] *Chronicon Paschale* (*Pat. Graec.*, XCII, 238); *De Orte et Obitu Patrum*, xxxi (*Pat. Lat.*, LXXXIII, 139).

[5] E.g., Clement of Alexandria, *Stromata*, I, xxi (*Pat. Graec.*, VIII, 838); Paulinus of Nola, *Poema XXIV*, lines 599-686 (*Pat. Lat.*, LXI, 626ff.); and Cyril of Alexandria, *Contra Julianum*, I (*Pat. Graec.*, LXXVI, 519).

[6] In *Two Letters concerning Virginity*, II, ix, trans., B. L. Pratten (*Ante-Nicene Christian Library* [Edinburgh, 1874], XIV, 389f.), Clement speaks of Samson as "the man of great strength . . . a Nazarite . . . consecrated to God . . . whom a woman brought to ruin with her wretched body, and her vile passion." Then, arguing from the *topos* of more and less, Clement wagged a warning finger at his reader: "Art thou, perchance, such a man as he? Know thyself, and know the measure of thy strength."

preachers did the same from that time on. In the fourth century Ambrose wrote a lengthy homily in the form of an epistle to his friend Vigilius, Bishop of Trient, in which Samson's entire career is reviewed to demonstrate the evils of marriage between Christian and infidel. Ambrose made it plain that even his being a Nazarite consecrated to God, attended by the Holy Spirit, and endowed with superhuman strength and zeal did not save Samson from the perils and sorrows lying in wait for him who takes an alien woman in marriage.[7] In his *Dittochaeum*, Prudentius derived a moral from the fountain which sprang from the jawbone and from Samson's discovery of honey in the carcass of the lion:

> Ab ore leonis
> Mella fluunt: maxilla asini fontem vomit ultro.
> Stultitia exundat lymphis, dulcedine virtus.[8]

Commentators who interpreted literally the story of Sam-

---

[7] *Epistola XIX* (*Pat. Lat.*, XVI, 1026-36). In the *Apologia* Ambrose used Samson as an example of a man strong in everything but mastery of passion: "Samson validus et fortis leonem suffocavit, sed amorem suum suffocare non potuit."

[8] *Pat. Lat.*, LX, 98f. This sort of tropological interpretation was not widely applied until the sixteenth century. In the seventh century Samson was brought into the liturgy in a moving and dramatic recounting of the latter part of his story included in the *Liturgia Mozarabica* (*Pat. Lat.*, LXXXV, 348-50). This version in detailed, simple, exciting liturgical style exploited to the full the interest and suspense of a good story. The emphasis is placed entirely on Samson's fall and catastrophe, the treatment of the attempts of Dalila to learn the secret of Samson's strength being one of its most interesting scenes. But every part of the action is vividly imagined and poetically expanded. An excerpt in translation will serve to indicate the power of this liturgical use of Samson, a version, be it remembered, which reached a large audience. "When the Philistines saw him they put out his eyes. And they led him into Gaza in chains. And they cast him in prison to labor at the mill. And in time his hair began to grow again. And the princes of the Philistines gathered together in order to worship their god Dagon. And they feasted saying: the Lord delivered our enemy Samson into our hands. And when the people saw this they praised their god saying: our god brought our enemy into our hands. Him who laid waste our land. And killed many. . . . But Samson, calling upon God, said: Lord God, remember me. And restore to me now my strength as of old, O my God! So that I may avenge myself against my enemies. . . . And he thrust himself violently against the columns. And the house fell upon all the princes and the multitude which was therein. And he killed many more at his death than he had during all the rest of his life."

son in the Book of Judges also interpreted literally his inclusion in the eleventh chapter of the Epistle to the Hebrews, where he was numbered among the patriarchs of the Old Testament, men who were all saints in the Pauline sense, that is, *electi*, true believers, men distinguished by their great faith. There was, to be sure, a great deal in the account of Samson in Judges which supported the belief that he was a saint. His birth was foretold by an angel of God, who promised that he would be consecrated to God and would undertake the deliverance of God's chosen people,[9] and many writers in the patristic period called attention to the fact that Samson was impelled and strengthened throughout his career by the Holy Spirit.[10] Furthermore, it was the opinion of Origen, Theodoret, and Procopius that a prophecy of Samson had been intended by Jacob when he said: "Dan shall judge his people, as one of the tribes of Israel."[11] But it is in the *Ad Episcopos Ægyptii et Libyae Epistola* of Athanasius (d. 373) that we find the earliest explicit indication that Christian thinkers would take up Samson as a saint, for in that work Athanasius spoke of David, Samuel, and Samson together as ἅγιοι, saints or holy men, who had always been revered because they wrought deeds of righteousness through faith and because they suffered death for their devotion to God.[12] In one of his homilies Chrysostom defended the inclusion of Samson among the holy fathers of the Old Testament, arguing that the less savory events of his life do not matter because he believed and was

[9] See, for example, Ambrose, *Epistola XIX* (*Pat. Lat.*, XVI, 1027f.).

[10] Vulgate: "Coepitque Spiritus Domini esse cum eo in castris Dan" (13:25); "Irruit autem Spiritus Domini in Samson" (14:16). Cf. Ambrose, *De Spiritu Sancto* (*Pat. Lat.*, XVI, 774ff.); Diodorus of Tarsus, *In Librum Judicum* (*Pat. Graec.*, XXXIII, 1587f.); Augustine, *Sermon 364*, paragraph 1 (*Pat. Lat.*, XXXIX, 1639); Cyril of Alexandria, *De Sancta et Consubstantiali Trinitate Dialogus VI* (*Pat. Graec.*, LXXV, 1094), and *In Librum Judicum Homiliae VIII* (*Pat. Graec.*, LXXV, 1131).

[11] Genesis 49:16. See Origen, *Commentarii in Evangelium Joannis*, VI, 12 (*Pat. Graec.*, XIV, 238f.); Theodoret, *Quaestiones in Genesin*, XLIX (*Pat. Graec.*, LXXX, 222); Procopius, *Commentarii in Genesin* (*Pat. Graec.*, LXXXVII, 503f.).

[12] *Pat. Graec.*, XXV, 588 b.

resplendent in faith.[13] And Augustine grouped Moses, Daniel, and Samson together as "patres nostri" who had risen up against false gods.[14] Of course, this conception of Samson as a saint gave point to the use of Samson as an example in the *a fortiori* arguments in favor of chastity already referred to.

There was one question, however, which troubled the Church Fathers in their acceptance of Samson as a saint. He had brought about his own death. Was he to be regarded as a suicide, and, if so, was his act of self-destruction to be taken as a pattern for true believers? Augustine answered this question very carefully in a chapter of his *De Civitate Dei* headed, "De his quae fieri non licent, cum a sanctis facta noscuntur, qua ratione facta credenda sint," in which he used Samson for the purpose of proving his contention that the saints are not necessarily to be imitated in *all* their acts. Nevertheless, he justifies Samson's self-destruction: it was an exceptional case because we know that Samson was impelled by God. And Augustine makes it clear that, although it is not for us to imitate the actions of saints indiscriminately, we may not question those actions done "divinitus jussae" and in obedience to God's will.[15] Augustine also defended Samson against the charge of murder on the same ground: he killed Philistines because the Holy Spirit moved within him, compelling him to serve God against idolaters.[16] It is especially significant, however, that Augustine did not in either connection call Samson's sanctity into question; the whole difficulty of interpreting and excusing his suicide and homicide lay in the very firmness of his position as a saint.

Although he was generally taken to be a saint, it was evident to most of the commentators of the patristic period that Samson had also fallen, at least temporarily, from saintly ways. Theodoret, in the fifth century, was troubled enough about his irregular career to ask how it was possible for Sam-

[13] *Enarratio in Epistolam ad Hebraeos Homilia XXVII* (*Pat. Graec.*, LXIII, 186f.).
[14] *Sermo de Tempore Barbarico* (*Pat. Lat.*, XL, 702f.).
[15] I, xxvi (*Pat. Lat.*, XLI, 39f.).
[16] *Ibid.*, col. 35.

son, after having lived dissolutely, to attain spiritual grace.[17]
To be sure, Theodoret readily found an answer to his question. He argued that all the apparent moral failures of Samson were, like his marrying the alien woman of Timnath, *a
Domino*, allowable by God's concessions and for God's own
purposes. But other writers were unable to answer the question with ease. Josephus had acknowledged that Samson fell
and had given four reasons for his fall: (1) he was "allured
and besotted by a woman," (2) he partook of "humane nature, which . . . cannot resist sinne," (3) "he transgressed the
ordinance of his fathers, and corrupted his domesticall manner of living, conforming himself to the fashions of the Gentiles," and (4) he was "more elate . . . then he ought to have
been," attributing his victories to his own "vertue" and "confessing not that it was done by the assistance of God."[18] The
interesting suggestion of *hybris* in the fourth of these reasons
was reinforced later by Gregory the Great, who remarked that
Samson's fall was preceded by the Christian version of *hamartia*, or "mentis caecitas," as he termed it, which is the inevitable
result of sin.[19] But other commentators in the patristic period
followed Jerome, who attributed Samson's fall to his having
defiled his sanctity with lust after womankind: "Sanctifica-
tionem capillorum ejus Dalilae libido turpavit."[20]

[17] *Quaestiones in Judices*, XXI (*Pat. Graec.*, LXXX, 510).
[18] *Antiquities*, V, x, trans. Lodge (London, 1640), pp. 120-23. In the
"Loeb Classics" edition of the *Antiquities*, Marcus renders the phrase
μεῖζον ἢ χρὴ ἐπὶ τούτῳ φρονῶν as "unduly proud of this feat" (p. 136f.).
[19] "Sciendum est quod aliquando prius oculus intellectus obtunditur, et
postmodum captus animus per exteriora desideria vagatur, ut caeca mens
quo ducitur nesciat, et carnis suae illecebris sese libenter subdat. . . . Tes-
tatur Samson ab Allophylis captus, qui postquam oculos perdidit, ad molam
deputatus est, quia nimirum maligni spiritus, postquam tentationum stimu-
lis intus aciem contemplationis effodiunt, foras in circuitum laborum mit-
tunt." This is to be found in the chapter of Gregory's *Moralia* headed:
"Peccandi consuetudo aliquando praeceditur mentis caecitate" (*Pat. Lat.*,
LXXV, 787). It is interesting in this connection to recall that Milton had
Samson blame his fall on an "impotence of mind" which made him "proud-
ly secure, yet liable to fall" (*Samson Agonistes*, lines 52-55).
[20] *Commentarii in Ezechielem Prophetam* (*Pat. Lat.*, XXV, 439f.). Cf.
Cyril of Alexandria (*Pat. Graec.*, LXXV, 1094), who says that God vanished
from Samson because he lusted after a harlot.

2

FROM the first, the commentators who endeavored to expound the story of Samson by means of literal interpretation were beset by difficulties. Origen, for example, adhered to literal interpretation as far as possible; however, he sometimes permitted himself slight but significant emendations in an effort to resolve inconsistencies or increase probability. An instance of this is his gloss of Judges 15:19—"But God clave an hollow place that was in the jaw, and there came water thereout." Origen emended this verse to read as follows: "He broke open the earth with a blow of the jawbone, and the waters gushed forth."[21] Augustine, too, was troubled by cruxes in the scriptural account of Samson and made early attempts at what might be called "philological" interpretation, by means of which he sought to preserve the literal sense with emendation and semantic sleight-of-hand.[22] At least one writer questioned, perhaps only rhetorically, whether Samson could have killed a thousand men with the jawbone of an ass and whether a fountain could have sprung from that weapon after he had thrown it down.[23]

Confronted with the wondrous and inconsistent story of a lusty folk-hero of the ancient Hebrews who had been accepted as a saint by the Christian Church, the early Fathers, seeking always to strengthen the bonds between the Old Testament and the New for the purpose of establishing the prescriptive unity of an immense body of divinely inspired Scripture, turned more and more often to non-literal interpretation. Allegory afforded them a satisfying solution. The Fathers adopted it early, and it gained steadily in prestige throughout the patristic period.

It is well known that allegorical interpretation originated in Greece with Homeric criticism and that it persisted, in

[21] *Adnotationes in Judices* (*Pat. Graec.*, XVII, 38).
[22] *Quaestionum in Heptateuchum*, VII, l-lvi (ed. J. Zycha, *Corp. Scrip. Eccles. Lat.* [Vienna, 1895], XXVIII, 501-6).
[23] Nilus Abbas, *Peristeria*, XI, viii (*Pat. Graec.*, LXXIX, 914f.).

spite of Plato's censure of the method,[24] up to the beginning
of the Christian era. It was adopted by rabbinical theologians
early in the first century, especially by Philo of Alexandria.
But the earliest instance of its application to the Samson story
which I have been able to find is in the writings of Ambrose
in the fourth century. In his *Expositio Psalmi CXVIII* he said
that Samson's foxes carrying firebrands into the standing crops
of the Philistines "signified by a figure" that wicked men, and,
most of all, heretics, shout with unrestrained tongue.[25] But it
is in the same writer's *Expositio in Septem Visiones Libri Apocalypsis* that allegorical interpretation really takes its characteristic shape for the first time, for there Ambrose said that
by his locks of hair Samson was a figure of Christ. Indeed, he
added, all true believers cling to Christ, the head of the
Church, just as Samson's locks clung to his head.[26]

Once the pattern of allegorical interpretation had been
made, there was no limit to its usefulness in exegesis of the
story of Samson. It enabled commentators to get round a number of obstacles which had hindered full acceptance of Samson as a saint, to bring more of the Old Testament within the
ethic of Christianity, and to make it appear that the entire
history of the world had been one long, unbroken anticipation
of the Advent. By the end of the seventh century nearly every
incident in the story of Samson had been analyzed and made
to yield figurative significance which foretold the story of
Christ and His teaching.

Of all the Christian writers who, during the patristic period, perpetuated and elaborated the allegorical interpretation
of Samson,[27] none contributed more than Augustine, who ex-

[24] *Phaedrus*, 229 d.

[25] "Improbi ac fraudulenti homines et maxime heretici liberum linguam
habeant ad latrandum" (ed. M. Petschenig, *Corp. Scrip. Eccles. Lat.*, LXII,
251).

[26] "Samson Christum significat: per capillos vero omnes electi designan-
tur. Et sicut capilli adhaerent capiti, ita et omnes justi adhaerent Christo,
qui caput est omnium electorum suorum" (*Pat. Lat.*, XVII, 854). There is
also some trace of allegorical interpretation in Ambrose's *De Spiritu Sancto*
(*Pat. Lat.*, XVI, 774ff.).

[27] E.g., Jerome, *Commentarii in Epistolam ad Ephesios* (*Pat. Lat.*, XXVI,

ploited allegory most fully in his *Sermo de Samsone*. Here
he established the following parallels: Samson in his strength
signifies Christ the Son of God, in his weakness, Christ the
Son of Man; Samson's riddle foreshadows the Resurrection
of Christ; the companion to whom Samson's bride was given
is a warning of the rise of heretics leading the Church from
Christ; Samson's having his strength in his hair is a figure of
Christ sustained by the prophecies of the Old Testament; and
Samson's hair growing again prophesies the conversion of the
Jews. Of all the parallels which Augustine constructed, however, the most significant was the one based on Samson's going
in unto the harlot in Gaza (Judges 16:1). This incident had
long troubled the commentators, and Augustine himself seems
to have been aware that, taken literally, it was a blot on Samson's record, and that, if he could interpret it allegorically,
it could be treated as a prophetic "darke conceit."[28] The next
of Samson's actions suggested a solution: in the middle of the
night Samson rose up and went out of the city, carrying away
the gates and their very bolts to a hill near Hebron. Augustine seized upon this incident as a figure of Christ's harrowing
of Hell, and it followed from this that the going in unto the
harlot could be construed as a figure of Christ lying in the
bonds of death:

Infernum et amorem mulieris, utrumque Scriptura conjungit. Inferni imaginem tenebat domus meretricis. Recte pro inferis poni-
tur: quia neminem repellit, et omnem intrantem ad se trahit. . . .
Ergo quod intravit, omnes viderunt, quod surrexit, pauci cog-
noverunt, tenuerunt, et palpaverunt. Tollit tamen portas civitatis,
id est, aufert portas inferni. Quid est portas inferni tollere, nisi

---

483f.), *Adversus Jovinianum* (*ibid.*, XXIII, 252f.), and *Commentarii in
Ezechielem Prophetam* (*ibid.*, XXV, 439f.); Paulinus of Nola, *Epistola
XXIII* (*Pat. Lat.*, LXI, 263-71); Procopius, *Commentarii in Judices* (*Pat.
Graec.*, LXXXVII, 1248); Gregory the Great, *XL Homiliae in Evangelia*
(*Pat. Lat.*, LXXVI, 1173f.), and *Moralia* (*Pat. Lat.*, LXXVI 490f.); and
Paterius' rescension of Gregory's exegetical works, *Liber de Expositione
Veteris ac Novi Testamenti*, VI, iii-vii (*Pat. Lat.*, LXXIX, 788-90).
[28] "Quod autem intravit ad meretricem, si sine causa fecit, quicumque
fecit, immundus est: si autem propheta fecit, sacramentum est" (*Sermo
364, Pat. Lat.*, XXXIX, 1642).

mortis imperium removere? Recipiebat enim et non remittebat. Quid autem fecit Dominus noster Jesus Christus? Ablatis portis mortis, ascendit in cacumen montis. Novimus enim eum et resurrexisse, et in coelos ascendisse.[29]

The analogy is so clear and complete that it is evident that this sermon "de Samsone" is, in reality, a sermon on Christ.

Augustine developed allegorical interpretation further in other places. In his *Contra Faustium* he explained that when Samson killed the lion which rushed upon him on his way to Timnath we were vouchsafed a figure of Christ founding His Church among the Gentiles, and also that the honey found in the lion's mouth signified the sweetness of the Gospel in a harsh world.[30] Moreover, Augustine contributed yet another element to allegorical interpretation when he derived allegory from an etymology of Samson's name: Samson, he explained, means "Sol ipsorum," or "their sun," and is therein a prefiguring of Christ, called "Sol justitiae."[31]

But Augustine was only one of many writers who allegorized the person and the deeds of Samson. Attention must be called to Isidore of Seville, who, at the end of the patristic period, compiled, in his *Mysticorum Expositiones Sacramentorum*, a sort of *summa* of all the allegorical interpretation developed during the first seven centuries of Christianity.[32] Isidore devoted an entire chapter to Samson, who, as he said at the outset, "habet quiddam in typo gestum Christi." Samson, he tells us, was a figure of Christ in many respects. His birth was foretold by an angel; he was called "Nazaraeus"; he liberated Israel from her enemies; he pulled down the

---

[29] *Ibid.*, col. 1642f.

[30] XII, 32 (ed. J. Zycha, *Corp. Scrip. Eccles. Lat.* [Vienna, 1891], xxv, 360). This interpretation was repeated in the following century by Eugippius Africanus, *Thesaurus* (*Pat. Lat.*, LXII, 679f.).

[31] *Enarrationes in Psalmos* (*Pat. Lat.*, XXXVII, 1041). This etymology of the name was throughout the patristic period the accepted one. Cf. Isidore of Seville, *Etymologiae*, VII, vi (*Pat. Lat.*, LXXXII, 278f.). It seems to have originated in Jerome's *Commentarii in Epistolam ad Philemonem* (*Pat. Lat.*, XXVI, 644f.), where he said: "Totam Samson fabulam, ad veri solis (hoc quippe nomen ejus sonat) trahere sacramentum."

[32] All quotations from Isidore of Seville in this paragraph are from *Pat. Lat.*, LXXXIII, 389f.

temple of idolatry. But Isidore went into detail. The first fore-telling of Samson's birth by the angel resembles the foretelling of Christ's incarnation by the first of the prophets, and the second coming of the angel to Manoa and his wife is a figure of the Annunciation. When Samson killed the lion he prefigured Christ saying, "Rejoice, for I shall overcome the world." The honey taken from the mouth of the lion signifies the kings of this earth who roared against Christ but who bowed to the sweetness of the Gospel. And Samson was especially a type of Christ in that he was victorious over more in dying than in living. However, Isidore declares confidently that, in yielding to the allurements of Dalila, Samson did not prefigure Christ; in that weakness he signified the hypocrites, those who glory in the name of Christian even while their deeds belie their pretended faith. Indeed, the meaning of Samson's surrendering himself to Dalila and being shorn of his Nazarite's locks is that if we yield to woman, that is to the flesh, and surrender to the demands of passion, we shall be despoiled of the spirit. And thus Satan will make sport of the proud and sinful as the Philistines made sport of Samson, who—"ab Allophylis captus, postquam oculos perdidit, ad molam deputatus,"—is sinful Man snatched away by evil spirits after they gouge out the inward eye of spiritual insight with barbs of temptation and send Man forth into a round of weary labor. But the restoration of Samson's holy locks is a promise that he who repents will be restored to grace: "deinde cupiditatis ac luxuriae subversis columnis, victores hostes dejicit, et reparato certamine in finem fortissime de daemonibus triumphabit."[33]

This was the design of the allegorical interpretation of Samson during the first age of Christian exegesis. He was not, of course, the only personage of the Old Testament who was treated in this way, but no other seems to have been so often, so fully allegorized as was he.[34] Indeed, allegorical interpreta-

---

[33] Isidore's interpretation of Samson was taken over in its entirety by Bede in *Quaestiones super Librum Judicum*, vii (*Pat. Lat.*, XCIII, 428ff.).
[34] The following Old Testament characters were also treated as figures

tion of the saints of the Old Testament seems to have been most fully developed in connection with Samson. Perhaps this was because the course of his story happened to admit of many satisfying analogies with Christ from Annunciation to Resurrection. Allegory was very close to the heart of the age, and "Samson noster," as he was often called, was very close to the heart of allegory. This is one of the reasons why Samson became a figure of importance in the Western mind during the Middle Ages.

3

Not only was Samson a link between the worlds of the Old Testament and the New, helping to unify the Hebraic and Christian traditions; he was also one of the figures by means of which the Judaeo-Christian tradition embraced and absorbed the heritage of Paganism. The similarity between the story of Samson and the story of Hercules seems to have been noticed first in the time of Julius Caesar by Diodorus Siculus, who compared the warm baths with which the Sicilian nymphs refreshed Hercules to the fountain which sprang from the jawbone which Samson had used as a weapon.[35] In the latter part of the third century, Eusebius of Caesarea mentioned in his *Chronicorum Canonum* that the life of Samson had been compared by some with the life of Hercules, and in the following century Philastrius gave it as his opinion that the Greeks had stolen the concept of Samson from the Old Testament and named it Hercules.[36] But most early writers were content to elaborate the parallels between the two figures: for example, both opened their heroic careers with the slaying of lions; both were brought to ruin at last by women; both died voluntarily; and both were miraculously strong. Samson's fox-

---

of Christ: Abraham (*Pat. Lat.*, LXI, 359); Melchisedech (*ibid.*); Isaac (*ibid.*, XIV, 1061; XXXV, 1464; XXXVI, 245; XXXVIII, 133; XLI, 511; XLII, 852; LXI, 359); Jacob (*ibid.*, XIV, 856; XXXIX, 1765; LXI, 359; CLXVII, 526f.); Moses, Joshua, Job, David, Noah, Eli, Enoch, *et al.* (*ibid.*, CCXIX, 451).

[35] *Bibliotheca Historica*, IV, 23 (ed. F. Fogel [Leipzig, 1888], I, 432f.).

[36] Eusebius, *Chronicorum Canonum Libri Duo*, ed. Alfred Schoene (Berlin, 1866), II, 54f.; Philastrius, *Liber de Haeresibus* (*Pat. Lat.*, XII, 1122).

catching they compared with Hercules' capture of the Ery-
manthian boar, the Cretan bull, or the hind of Artemis. Samson's going into Gaza suggested Hercules' descent to Hell,
and Samson's carrying the gates of the city to the hill near
Hebron reminded the commentators of the setting up of the
pillars of Hercules. Samson and Hercules were so often compared or identified throughout the patristic period that their
association became a stock-feature of nearly all hermeneutic,
homiletic, or poetic references to Samson. Few writers ever
thought of one without being reminded of the other.[37]

During this first period of Christian exegesis, the principal
elements of the Samson tradition were compounded. As a
result of the working of both literal and allegorical interpretation, Samson was already a much more complex and significant concept of the Christian mind than one might have expected to grow from the intensely nationalistic folk tale in
which he was first found. This tribesman of Dan had come to
be regarded as the original of one of the most highly respected
of the Greek heroes, as a saint—albeit a saint who fell because
of pride or lust and who was restored to grace—and, most
important of all, as a figure of Christ. More was added to the
Samson tradition during succeeding centuries, but these were
the fundamental meanings of Samson in the Christian mind
up to the time of Milton.

[37] Augustine, *De Civitate Dei*, XVIII, xix (*Pat. Lat.*, XLI, 576f.); *Chronicon Paschale* (*Pat. Graec.*, XCII, 238); Georgius Syncellus, *Chronographia*
(ed. W. Dindorf [Bonn, 1829], I, 309). Cf. Moore, *Critical and Exegetical
Commentary on Judges* (New York, 1895), p. 364f., who gives a lengthy
bibliography of modern attempts to identify Samson and Hercules and to
trace their origin to the Phoenician myth of Melqart, or to the Egyptian
Horus-Ra. It is interesting to note that all such studies usually conclude, as
did Jerome, that Samson originated in a solar myth. Cf. the association of
Hercules and Christ (Hughes, *op.cit.*, p. 429), and see below, pp. 41-45, 59,
78f., 85, 130.

Chapter IV

THE SAMSON OF THE SCHOLASTIC PERIOD

AFTER the eighth century, much of the history of the Samson tradition appears to be repetition. Sometimes the repetition seems merely cumulative, but even cumulative repetition serves to enhance the authority of elements introduced during the earlier period. More often the repetition is incremental, so that a new significance accrues to its burden as a result of a changed context. Throughout the scholastic period there were changes in emphasis, too, which altered the meaning of Samson as part of the content of the Christian mind.

1

EVEN writers who adhered strictly to literal interpretation and merely repeated the Samson story without explicit commentary were unable to return to a version completely free from the connotations which the story had acquired during the patristic period.[1] Indeed, between the eighth and the fourteenth centuries literal interpretation seems to have been greatly weakened. At least there are very few writers in that period who, like Philip of Harveng or his predecessors among the Fathers, not only clung to the literal sense of the Samson story but particularly stressed the miraculous aspects of his life.[2] If there was a scholastic temper, it did not love to lose itself in an "O altitudo!" It seems to have preferred what was then taken to be historical truth, and it was during this

[1] E.g., Eutychius of Alexandria, *Annales* (*Pat. Graec.*, CXI, 937ff.), who repeated the story exactly as he found it in Judges but put greater emphasis on the end of Samson's career than on his earlier exploits. See also Petrus Comestor, *Liber Judicum*, xvi-xix, in *Historia Scholastica* (*Pat. Lat.*, CXCVIII, 1285-90), who brought the influence of Josephus into the Samson tradition. These two texts, however, are the only two in this period which compare with the earlier simple repetitions found in the writings of Sulpicius Severus, Paulinus of Nola, and Cyprian, or in the *Chronicon Paschale*.
[2] *De Obedientia Clericorum* (*Pat. Lat.*, CCIII, 926f.).

period that literal interpretation was directed principally at establishing even more firmly the historicity of such biblical figures as Samson. Georgius Hamartolus, Joannes Zonaras, and Petrus Comestor—the chroniclers and annalists of the day—placed Samson chronologically and magnified his importance as ruler and liberator of Israel.[3]

The perpetuation of the belief that Samson was a saint was, however, a far more significant consequence of literal interpretation. Although this conception flourished during the scholastic period, there were some hints of doubt. Rabanus Maurus, for example, remarked at the beginning of this period that "some have blamed Paul for naming Barach, Samson, and Jephtha here," but he answered immediately, "Quid dicis? meretricem ponit, istos non ponat?"—if the harlot Rahab can be named here, why not these others? And then he added his conviction that Barach, Samson, and Jephtha deserved mention here because they won glory by their faith.[4] This was the usual interpretation of Samson in all commentaries on the Epistle to the Hebrews. Haymo Halberstatensis, Atto of Vercelli, and Theophylactus of Bulgaria all made it clear that Samson and the others were cited in the Epistle to the Hebrews, not because they were good in all respects, but because they were resplendent with faith and thereby wrought great deeds. Theophylactus of Bulgaria was especially emphatic on this point, declaring that Samson, who was the most mighty of all in war, fought for, and brought about, justice.[5]

[3] Georgius Hamartolus, *Chronicon Breve* (*Pat. Graec.*, CX, 202); Joannes Zonaras, *Annales*, I, xxix (*Pat. Graec.*, CXXXIV, 118f.); and Petrus Comestor, *Historia Scholastica* (*Pat. Lat.*, CXCVIII, 1290). Cf. Ælfric, *Treatise on the Old and New Testament*, trans., Edward Thwaites (London, 1623), ed. S. J. Crawford, *EETS*, original series, no. 160 (London, 1922), p. 33f.; Georgius Cedrenus, *Compendium Historiarum* (*Pat. Graec.*, CXXI, 135-38); and Wyclif, *The Holy Bible*, ed. J. Forshall and F. Madden (Oxford, 1850), *in loc.* Judges 13.

[4] "Nec mihi nunc dicas aliam vitam eorum, sed si non crediderunt et si non claruerunt in fide." *Enarrationes in Epistolas Beati Pauli* (*Pat. Lat.*, CXII, 803f.).

[5] Haymo Halberstatensis, *In Divini Pauli Epistolas Expositio* (*Pat. Lat.*, CXVII, 912f.); Atto of Vercelli, *Expositio in Epistolas S. Pauli* (*Pat. Lat.*, CXXXIV, 811); Theophylactus of Bulgaria, *Expositio in Epistolam ad Hebraeos* (*Pat. Graec.*, CXXV, 362f.).

The most elaborate defense of his inclusion among the saints was written by Harvey of Burgundy in the twelfth century. Samson, he said, conquered kingdoms through faith; he was possessed of great strength because he had in him the spirit of God, which sustained him and enabled him to harass the Philistines. He wrought justice as well, for he judged Israel for twenty years. He was a Nazarite, consecrated to God from the very womb of his mother, and he was true to his Nazaritic vows, for he drank no wine and tasted no unclean thing. All his deeds were the work of the Holy Spirit; even his marriages with alien women were according to the will of God, although such alliances were prohibited by law, which God may abridge for His own purposes. Nor did Samson sin in destroying a multitude of his enemies and himself with them, because this, too, was really the work of the Holy Spirit, which empowered and impelled him. Harvey concluded that Paul had been fully justified in using Samson to exemplify those who achieved greatness through faith.[6] But it is clear from this testimony that Samson's deeds were forgiven only if he had been prompted inwardly by the Holy Spirit—as Peter Lombard said in this connection, "Nec Samson aliter excusatur quod ipsum cum hostibus ruina domus oppressit, nisi quia Spiritus latenter hoc jusserat."[7] More and more, towards the close of the scholastic period, this became a

---

[6] "Samson per fidem devicit regna, quia cum esset unus vir, sed haberet in se Spiritum Domini, qui confortabat eum, ingentes strages Philistaeorum multoties dedit, nullusque eorum fortitudinem habere poterat ut illi resisteret. Justitiam quoque operatus est, quia judicavit Israel viginti annis, et Philistaeos oppressores eorum afflixit, et Nazaraeus, id est consecratus fuit ex utero matris suae, vinum et siceram non bibens, et nihil immundum comedens. In fine tamen quo se cum hostibus oppressit, non aliter excusatur, nisi quia spiritus latenter hoc jusserat, qui per illum miracula faciebat, sicut et antea illi inspiraverat ut uxorem de filiabus Philistaeorum acciperet, cum lex hoc prohiberet. Nam, sicut in acceptione uxoris alienigenae fecit per voluntatem Dei, quod lex interdixerat, et non peccavit, ita credi potest quod Spiritus sanctus illi jusserit extinguere secum ingentem illam hostium multitudinem, quae de ejus humilitatione laudabat idolum suum, et ad majus improperium faciebat eum ebrium ludere, praesertim cum jam ille spiritus coepisset ei pristinas vires reddere, ad designationem recuperationis prioris gratiae. Unde et nunc Apostolus ponit eum inter eos, qui adepti sunt repromissiones" (*Pat. Lat.*, CLXXXI, 1658).

[7] *Collectanea in Epistolas Sancti Pauli* (*Pat. Lat.*, CXCII, 497).

question of importance affecting the position of Samson as a
saint. If prominent writers like Alanus ab Insulis had not
given it as their opinion that Samson killed himself and his
enemies only at God's instigation, his reputation would have
suffered greatly.[8] But the defense of Samson was well constructed by the time Thomas Aquinas considered his case.
Thomas stated the question simply and readily accepted all
the implications of it. It was his opinion that some are given
dispensation to kill themselves, and he cited Samson as an
example in his proof of this opinion: "Samson killed himself,
as we are told in Judges 16; however, Samson was numbered
among the saints, as is clear from Hebrews 11. Therefore it
is granted to some to kill themselves."[9] Of course, Thomas was
convinced that Samson's actions were prompted by the Holy
Spirit, but his justification of Samson's suicide did not depend
on that conviction.[10] Again, as earlier in Augustine's defense
of Samson, one notes that none of these writers in the scholastic period ever questioned Samson's sanctity itself. There is
only *ex silentio* indication that the justness of Samson's mention among the saints had ever been called into question;
and the many defenses of Samson—especially those by prominent writers like Rabanus Maurus, Alanus ab Insulis, and
Thomas Aquinas—made his position as a saint more secure
than it had ever been before.[11]

2

DURING the age of the Church Fathers, literal and allegorical interpretation had developed side by side; but most writ-

[8] "De Samsone dicimus, quod divina inspiratione se interfecit, et pecca-
tum quod antea forte fecerat, per mortem expiavit" (*De Fide Catholica
contra Haereticos* [*Pat. Lat.*, CCX, 343f.]).

[9] *Summa Theologiae*, II, ii, ques. 64, art. 5, paragraph 4 (Ottawa, 1942),
III, 1759b-1760a.

[10] He used Samson as an example in an article headed, "Utrum gradus
prophetiae possint distingui secundum visionem imaginariam." *Summa Theologiae*, II, ii, ques. 174, art. 3 (*loc.cit.*, III, 2283 a-b).

[11] Lanfranc of Canterbury, in his commentary on the Epistle to the
Hebrews (*Pat. Lat.*, CL, 401f.), justified Jephtha's being named in Hebrews
11 but said nothing in defense of Samson, Gideon, Barach, David, or Samuel—perhaps because he saw no reason to explain their inclusion.

ers, even those like Augustine, who used both methods of exegesis, kept them separated. In the age of the Schoolmen, the two methods were often used simultaneously to distinguish different levels of meaning. Ælfric was one who stated emphatically his conviction that we must interpret every word of the Samson story literally, accepting the marvels of his career as miracles wrought by God:

Nu gif hwa wundrie, hu hit gewurðan mihte þæt Samson se stranga swa ofslean mihte an þusend manna mid þaes assan cin bane, þonne secge se mann, hu þæt gewurðan mihte, þæt God him sende þa wæter of þæs assan teð. Nis þis nan gedwimor ne nan dwollic sagu, ac seo ealde gesetniss ys eall swa trumlic, swa swa se Hælend sæde in his halgan godspelle, þæt an stæf ne bið, ne an strica, awæged of ðære ealdan gesetnisse, þæt hi ne beon gefyllede: gif hwa ðises ne gelyfð, he ys ungeleafulic.[12]

He who does not believe in these miracles, who does not accept the words of the Scripture without altering a single letter or a single stroke, is no believer at all. And yet Ælfric freely adopted allegorical interpretation too, for in his commentary on Judges he remarked that in his death "Samson betokened our Savior, who by His own death overcame the Devil, triumphed over Satan's power, and redeemed mankind." He also gave an allegorical interpretation of Samson's carrying away the gates of Gaza: this signifies Christ harrowing Hell.[13] The two interpretations might be thought to be mutually exclusive, but apparently they were not so regarded in the scholastic period.

The widely influential Rabanus Maurus had made use of both literal and allegorical interpretation in the ninth century. In his *Commentarii in Librum Judicum et Ruth*, he devoted five chapters to a discussion of Samson. This commentary, like the *Glossa Ordinaria* of Walafrid Strabo in the same century, is an omnium gatherum of all previous exegesis.[14] In both of

---

[12] *The Old English Version of the Heptateuch*, ed. S. J. Crawford, *EETS*, original series, no. 160 (Oxford, 1922), p. 411.

[13] *Ibid.*, p. 414.

[14] Rabanus Maurus, *Commentarii in Librum Judicum et Ruth* (*Pat. Lat.*, CVIII, 531f.). Strabo's gathering of all patristic commentary is especially significant because it was reprinted as a marginal gloss in Nicholas de Lyra's

these books literal and allegorical interpretations are combined. Rabanus Maurus seems always to have gone as far as possible with literal and grammatical annotation before he turned to Alexandrian allegory, but the dominant effect of his exposition is allegorical nevertheless. His comment on Samson is one of the most detailed in the Middle Ages, and one of the least original.[15]

Allegorical interpretation is to be found in nearly all commentaries dealing with Samson in the period of the Schoolmen. In the ninth century it is not only in the writings of Rabanus Maurus and Walafrid Strabo, but also in the *Expositio in Matthaeum* of Paschasius Radbertus; in the eleventh century Peter Damiani construed Samson's foxes as a figure of heresy and the jawbone as a figure of Christ.

But the most interesting developments in allegorical interpretation are to be found in twelfth- and thirteenth-century writings.[16] Rupert of St. Heribert (d. 1135) wrote a very minute and complete commentary on Judges which is entirely allegorical. He was particularly ingenious in discerning parallels between Samson and Christ, and consequently his *Commentarii in Librum Judicum* is a *locus classicus* of allegorical exegesis of the Samson story in the late Middle Ages.[17] He repeated all the parallels which had been suggested by earlier writers, and he added many new parallels of his own. He, too, set out from the assumption that Samson's feats were miracles: "Samson hujus Nazaraei fortissimi omnes sunt actus mirabiles, manifestum in se divinae virtutis vel fortitudinis opus exprimentes. Neque enim opera sunt hominis, sed Dei." Rupert divided Samson's career to make seven main events, which,

---

Biblia Sacra cum Glossis, at the beginning of the sixteenth century, giving the Renaissance biblical scholar ready access to the exegesis of the early Church Fathers.

[15] See also his allegorical etymologies in *De Universo* (*Pat. Lat.*, CXI, 57): "Samson interpretatur *sol eorum*, vel *sol fortitudo*. . . . Dalila . . . interpretatur *paupercula*, vel *situla*."

[16] Paschasius Radbertus, *Expositio in Matthaeum* (*Pat. Lat.*, CXX, 929); Peter Damiani, *Collectanea in Vetus Testamentum* (*Pat. Lat.*, CXLV, 1089f.), and *Sermon* LXVIII (*Pat. Lat.*, CXLIV, 892f.).

[17] *Pat. Lat.*, CLXVII, 1041-55.

like his seven locks of hair, signified the seven sacraments, or
the seven last words of Christ on the Cross. He perpetuated
the analogy between the angel's foretelling the birth of Samson and the Annunciation. The lion which rushed upon Samson in the road to Timnath was equivalent to Satan tempting
Christ in the wilderness. The standing crops of the Philistines
destroyed by Samson's foxes symbolized the works of the
Jews, the studies of the Scribes, the heritage of the Pharisees.
The jawbone of the ass which Samson wielded in battle was
a prefiguring of the clear, simple gospel of Christ. Samson's
bearing away the gates of Gaza and going up on the hill near
Hebron was a figure of Christ harrowing Hell and ascending
into Heaven. Rupert devised an elaborate allegory to explain
in detail the full significance of the bonds with which Dalila
at first bound Samson. His treatment of Samson's story became more detailed as he approached its catastrophic conclusion. He made Dalila's betrayal of Samson correspond to
Judas' betrayal of Christ. The blinding of Samson was a
figure of Christ's agony in Gethsemane, and Samson's death
in the temple of Dagon was a figure of Christ crucified. Most
of the features of this allegory Rupert found already current
in the Samson tradition as he inherited it from his predecessors, but the division of Samson's works into seven principal
episodes, the analysis of the meaning of Dalila's bonds, and
the parallels between the lion and the temptation of Christ,
between the foxes and the Jews, between the blinding of Samson and the agony of Christ, and between Samson's death beside the pillars and Christ's death on the Cross—all these
seem to have been his own contribution.

Although Rupert of St. Heribert contributed more than
anyone else in the scholastic period to the allegorical interpretation of Samson, he also raised a question which might
have destroyed it. It has already been pointed out that Origen,
Theodoret, and Procopius assumed Samson to be the fulfillment of the prophecy of Jacob: "Dan shall judge his people,
as one of the tribes of Israel" (Genesis 49:16). But no one
before Rupert seems to have faced squarely the full signifi-

The Samson of the Scholastic Period 53

cance of this prophecy. Jacob had said more about Dan in the following verse: "Dan shall be a serpent by the way, an adder in the path, that biteth the horse heels, so that his rider shall fall backward." Rupert considered both the literal and allegorical senses of this passage and concluded that Jacob must have intended a prophecy of Samson. He paraphrased Jacob's words: "Nunc video in Spiritu comam nutrire Samson Nazaraeum tuum, caesis hostibus triumphare, quod in similitudinem colubri regulisque obsidentis vias nullum per terram Israel transire permittat."[18] This prophecy was, he thought, a description "per metaphoram" of Samson's harassing the Philistines. But contemplation of the works of Samson drew from Rupert a doubt which might have shaken the framework of the entire allegorical tradition: "Videns ergo tam fortem Nazaraeum tuum, quod et ipse propter meretricem mortuus est, et mortuos nostros occidit inimicos, putavi, O Deus, ipsum esse Christum, Filium tuum?" Can such a one, who consorted with a whore and was a ruthless killer, be thought to be our Lord, Jesus Christ, the Son of God? Rupert wondered whether Samson's deeds could be reconciled at all with Christian ethics. He recalled Samson's behavior on the battlefield after he had inflicted woeful defeat on his enemies: Samson thought only of himself and of his own need, and "nunquid enim verus Samson Christus Dominus, istos deseruit morientes, aut in ipsa morte projecit, ut desereret mortuos, per quos viventes pugnavit et vicit." He contrasted Samson with St. Peter, who, Rupert remembered, was no senator, no conqueror, no military hero, but only a humble fisherman. Indeed, he reflected, some have taken Jacob's prophecy of the serpent in the way to signify Antichrist, and Samson was of the tribe of Dan and a serpent in the way. It is impossible to be sure whether he was presenting his own opinion in disguise under the formula common throughout the Middle Ages for the expression of one's own

<hr>

[18] All quotations from Rupert in this paragraph are from his *Commentarii in Genesin* (*Pat. Lat.*, CLXVII, 556f.), and his *De Operibus Spiritus Sancti* (*Pat. Lat.*, CLXVII, 1742).

thoughts as the thoughts of others. Nor does this question happen to be of great importance here.

It is true that in the next generation a form of interpretation developed which gained increasing favor over allegory in the period following that of the Schoolmen. In his *Allegoriae in Vetus Testamentum*, Hugo of St. Victor (d. 1173) interpreted Samson as a figure of Christ in a number of respects: Samson overcame the lion, and Christ triumphed over Satan; Samson took honey from the lion's mouth, and Christ saved Man from the Devil; Samson married a Philistine, and Christ founded his Church among the Gentiles.[19] But in his commentary on Jeremiah, Hugo devised another sort of figurative interpretation of Samson. Here the interpretation is mystical: "Samson . . . significat animum divina cognitione illuminatum. Caput Samsonis principale est mentis. Capillus capitis radius est contemplationis." Samson was unconquerable as long as his locks—the rays of mystical insight—were preserved. But having lost the inner light of divine contemplation Samson was the easy prey of woman and of the allurement of fleshly lust.[20] In the same period a more obscure writer, Thomas Cisterciensis, after listing the principal parallels between Samson and Christ, declared that "Samson est spiritus humanus, Philisthiim daemones."[21] Although there is no demonstrable relationship between these allegories in anagogical terms and the misgivings about allegory expressed by Rupert of St. Heribert, and although allegorical interpretation of Samson as a figure of Christ persisted after the twelfth century[22] and throughout the Renaissance with undiminished vigor, this turning aside from allegorical interpretation on the part of the Victorines does foreshadow the tendency towards anagogical and tropological exegesis during the Reformation.

3

THROUGHOUT the scholastic period there were changes of

[19] *Pat. Lat.*, CLXXV, 680.   [20] *Pat. Lat.*, CLXXV, 263.
[21] *In Cantica Canticorum Eruditissimi Commentarii* (*Pat. Lat.*, CCVI, 59f.).
[22] E.g., Alanus ab Insulis, *Sermones Octo* (*Pat. Lat.*, CCX, 211f.).

emphasis in the Samson literature which carried the tradition ever nearer the treatment of Samson in Milton's tragedy. More attention was given to the later part of Samson's life and, therefore, to his fallen state. His status as a saint was not questioned, but the cause of his fall was frequently inquired into. For this reason Dalila came to occupy a position of greater importance in the Samson literature, and greater emphasis was placed upon her attempts to learn the secret of his strength.[23] Interest was drawn away from Samson's earlier sensational feats, and increasing interest was given instead to Samson's betrayal, his capture, his blindness, his ignominy in the hands of the Philistines, his labors at the mill, and his death.[24] There are two especially interesting twelfth-century writings in which this change of emphasis is exemplified. One is a sermon by the obscure Godefridus Admontensis; the other is a poem by Peter Abelard.

Perhaps the tradition of allegorical interpretation suggested to Godefridus Admontensis that he devote a Palm Sunday sermon to Samson and Dalila. For whatever reason, it is certain that he did choose to preach such a sermon; and it is equally certain that he succeeded in making this sermon "De Samsone et Dalila" perfectly suitable for the occasion. He opened quietly:

Dies ista, fratres charissimi, bene nominatur dies palmarum, in qua Rex et Dominus noster Jesus Christus, ut triumpharet de diabolo, et palmam victoriae reportaret, hodie vexilla crucis dignatus est levare, et ad locum passionis et certaminis tanquam pugil fortissimus et gloriosus properare.[25]

---

[23] Eutychius of Alexandria, *Annales* (*Pat. Graec.*, CXI, 937ff.); Petrus Comestor, *Historia Scholastica* (*Pat. Lat.*, CXCVIII, 1285-90); Godefridus Admontensis, "Homilia XLII: in Dominicam in Palmis Quarta: Samsone et Dalila" (*Pat. Lat.*, CLXXIV, 275-88).

[24] Georgius Hamartolus, *Chronicon Breve* (*Pat. Graec.*, CX, 202f.); Eutychius of Alexandria, *Annales* (*ibid.*, CXI, 937ff.); Theophylactus of Bulgaria, *Expositio in Epistolam ad Hebraeos* (*ibid.*, CXXV, 362f.); Hugo of St. Victor, *Adnotationibus Elucidatoriae in Threnos Jeremiae* (*Pat. Lat.*, CLXXV, 263); Thomas Cisterciensis, *In Cantica Canticorum* (*ibid.*, CCVI, 59f.); and Peter Abelard, "Planctus Israel super Samson," in *Planctus Varii* (*ibid.*, CLXXVIII, 1820f.).

[25] All quotations from Godefridus are from his *Homilia XLII* (*Pat. Lat.*, CLXXIV, 275-88).

Continuing, he reminded his listeners that the whole Christian Story had been prefigured by the life of Samson, who, "veri Nazaraei, de utero matris consecrati, Domini nostri Jesu Christi formam praetulit et habuit, ac per mirabilem fortitudinem suam divinae fortitudinis et virtutis opus exprimebat." Then Godefridus moved on into the main body of his sermon. He took up the story of Samson with the beginning of his association with Dalila and related only this latest part of Samson's life. He developed very fully the episode wherein Dalila tried to learn the secret of Samson's strength. He skillfully built up the rise of emotion throughout, achieved a moving climax in relating Samson's death, and reached a resounding close—"per infinita saecula saeculorum. Amen." The sermon is a fabric of allegorical interpretation, not a dispassionate rationalization of analogies, but an inspired, poetical *discordia concors*. Of the blinding of Samson, Godefridus said, "Evulsi sunt oculis Samsonis; evulsi sunt et oculi veri Samsonis, ex utero consecrati, Domini Salvatoris." Of Samson's being led as a captive to Gaza, he said, "Ductus est et Christus Gazam, dum ad aram crucis ducitur est immolandus pro nobis." Worshippers in 1949 would be surprised, and perhaps displeased with their minister, if he chose to preach about Samson and Dalila on Palm Sunday. It would seem to most of us today a breach of homiletic propriety, for we have lost the allegorical tradition completely and are not accustomed to thinking of Samson as the counterpart of Christ.

Peter Abelard (1079-1142) wrote a number of hymns and a remarkable series of *Planctus*, or lamentations, on subjects taken from the Old Testament. One of these is a *Planctus Israel super Samson* of eighty-seven lines. The tone of the whole poem is suggestive of tragedy, instinct as it is with the idea of the ruin of a great man:

> O semper fortium
> Ruina maximam,
> Et in exitium
> Creatam feminam!
> Haec patrem omnium,

> Dejecit protinus,
> Et mortis poculum,
> Propinat omnibus.
>> David sanctior
>> Salomone prudentior
>>> Quis putetur?
>> Aut quis ineptus
>> Magis per hanc fatuus
>>> Reperitur?
>> Quis ex fortibus
>> Sicut Samson fortissimus
>>> Enervatur? [26]

As a result of these changes of emphasis during the scholastic period—centering attention upon Dalila's betrayal of Samson and upon Samson's fall and catastrophe—the story was carried ever further from its origin in naïve racial folklore, ever nearer to its culmination in tragedy. More and more the story took on tragic form as the writers who handled it turned it into the account of a great man, a saint, a counterpart of Hercules, a type of Christ, who falls from happiness to misery.

But there was still another consequence of these changing emphases which had a more immediate effect on the literature which accumulated around the figure of Samson. It naturally followed that, as attention was called to the part which she had played in Samson's downfall, Dalila would be more frequently an object of censure. Abelard blamed her for Samson's blindness:

> Quem primum Dalila
> Sacra caesarie,
> Hunc hostes postea
> Privarunt lumine.

And he heaped shame upon her for her perfidy.

> Ludos martios
> Plus exercere solitos
>> Frangit artus.
>> Quid tu, Dalila,

---

[26] *Pat. Lat.*, CLXXVIII, 1820f. The reference to David here seems to indicate that his escapades made Samson's harlotry more acceptable.

Quid ad haec elicis impia?
Quid fecisti, quaenam munera,
Per tanta tibi scelera conquiris?

There is the same malignment of the woman of Sorek in the *Epigrammata* of Theodorus Prodromus, seven of whose twenty epigrams on Samson are devoted to denigration of Dalila.[27]

In the interim between the highest development of Scholasticism and the apex of the Renaissance, the secular poetic tradition built upon the story of Samson, which had its beginning in the *Planctus* of Abelard, was taking definite form. The characteristic shape of all secular poetic treatments of Samson in the late Middle Ages was the result of changes in emphasis wrought by commentators during the preceding period. As attention was directed more and more to the latter part of Samson's life, his history came to be thought of as a tragedy in the medieval sense. But at the same time, as has been shown, attention was also directed to Dalila. Consequently, when Samson's story was told in secular poetry, it was presented as a great man's fall from happiness to misery resulting from the perfidy of a woman.

The Samson story appeared in English literature at the opening of the fourteenth century in the *Cursor Mundi*.[28] This is a purely secular version of the story: all the religious elements are omitted. There is no mention of the foretelling of Samson's birth by an angel, of his being a Nazarite, of his serving God's cause against the Philistines, no suggestion of a conflict between God and Dagon. Whatever the significance of the *Cursor Mundi* as a whole may be, the story of Samson is there used as a spirited, fast-moving tale, an absorbing story of a man and a woman. The author seems to have avoided the religious aspects of the story: he even has Dalila marry another Philistine after her betrayal of Samson, so that it is at her wedding-feast that Samson pulls down the columns:

[27] *Pat. Graec.*, CXXXIII, 1142-46.
[28] Lines 7083-7262, ed. Richard Morris, *EETS*, original series, nos. 57 and 59 (London, 1874), pp. 410-21.

Whenne he was done in prisoun
A mon of þat same nacioun
Gat dalida his wyf to wedde.
Sampson was to þe bridale ledde. . . .
Bi a piler was his sete
To myrþe men at her mete
whenne þei were gladdest at þe feest
Sampson coude wel geest
Somdel waxen was his here
þe post þat al þe hous vp bere
wiþ boþe his hondes he hit shoke
So fast þat al þe hous quoke
þe hous he falde ȝaf no mon griþ
his foos he slouȝe him self þer wiþ.

Near the end of the same century Chaucer, too, retold the
story of Samson in the *Monk's Tale*,[29] where, again, the religious elements, though not omitted, are subordinated, and
Samson is treated as the type of a man endowed with great
physical strength but deficient in prudence.

Was nevere swich another as was hee,
To speke of strengthe, and therwith hardynesse;
But to his wyves toolde he his secree,
Thurgh which he slow hymself for wrecchednesse.

In this version of the story, as in the *Cursor Mundi*, the interest is focused on the good-man-bad-woman plot. Although
Samson "hadde of Israel the governaunce," Dalila brought
him "to meschaunce." Samson properly belonged in the
Monk's sermon *de casibus virorum illustrium*; like Lucifer,
Adam, and Hercules, in whose company he is found here, he
was a great one who fell from happiness to misery.

But now is he in prison in a cave,
Where-as they made hym at the queerne grynde.
O noble Sampsoun, strongest of mankynde,
O whilom juge, in glorie and richesse!
Now maystow wepen with thyne eyen blynde,
Sith thou fro wele art falle in wrecchednesse.[30]

[29] Lines 2015-94, ed. F. N. Robinson (Boston and New York, 1933),
p. 226f.
[30] The Monk gave much more space to Samson than to Lucifer, Adam,
or Hercules. See also Chaucer's other references to Samson in *Wyf of Bath's*

The emphases which appeared early in the *Cursor Mundi* and in the poetry of Chaucer persisted throughout the secular literature about Samson in the fifteenth century. In the *Confessio Amantis* of John Gower, Samson is treated as one "whos love his strengthe al overthrewe," who, although he was one of "the moste wise," was "of love adoted":

> Love is of so grete a main,
> That where he takth an herte on honde,
> Ther mai nothing his myht withstonde:
> The wise Salomon was nome,
> And strong Sampson overcome.[31]

When John Lydgate paraphrased in English Laurent de Premierfait's French version of Boccaccio's *De Casibus Virorum Illustrium*, he headed the section dealing with Samson as follows: "Off myghty Sampson whiche tolde his counsaile to Dalida wherby he was deceived." As this heading indicates, Lydgate, too, shaped the material to make a story about Samson and Dalila and dealt mainly with the latter part of Samson's life. He reviewed rapidly the earlier deeds of Samson and devoted most of his account to Dalila's treachery and to Samson's subsequent death.

> And in a vale which callid was Soret
> Ful hoote he loued Dalida the faire. . . .
> But I dar calle hir Dalida the double,
> Cheeff roote & cause off al his mortal trouble.[32]

Lydgate (following Boccaccio and Premierfait) related in great detail the attempts of Dalila to learn the secret of

---

Prologue, lines 719-26 (where the Wyf denies that "womman was the los of al mankynde"); in *Man of Law's Tale*, lines 197-203; in *Pardoner's Tale*, lines 565-87; and in *Book of the Duchess*, lines 738-39 (where it is said that Samson died because of Dalila).

[31] VI, iii, 4, and VIII, iii, 366, in *English Works*, ed. G. C. Macaulay, *EETS*, extra series, no. 82 (London, 1901), II, 169f., 459.

[32] Lydgate's references to Samson are found in the *Fall of Princes*, I, 6335-6510, 6616-22; III, 1184-90, 1597-1603; VIII, 155-61 (ed. Henry Bergen, *EETS*, extra series, nos. 121-23 [London, 1924], pp. 179-84, 187, 361, 373, 827); and in *Troy Book*, I, 1861-72 (ed. Henry Bergen, *EETS*, extra series, no. 97 [London, 1906], p. 67).

Samson's strength, when she, "lich a serpent daryng vnder floures," tempted him with

> fair pretense
> Off trewe menyng vnder fals apparence.

He drew a complete contrast between Samson, who "mente trouth," who was "feithful" and "stedfast," and Dalila, who was "variable," "ontrewe," and "onstable."

> Thus Sampson was be Dalida deceyued,
> She coude so well flatre, forge and fayne.

And in the "Envoye" Lydgate spoke of Samson's history as a "tragedie" meant to warn princes to

> Keep your conceitis vnder couerture,
> Suffre no nyhtwerm withynne your counsail kreepe,
> Thouh Dalida compleyne, crei and weepe!

It can be seen from such non-ecclesiastical texts as those just reviewed that the story of Samson was thoroughly secularized and fully exploited in poetry before the beginning of the Renaissance in England. The typical poetic treatment of Samson in medieval English literature, as distinguished from the typical scholastic treatment, subordinated, or completely eliminated, the religious significance of his story and shaped it as a tragedy in which a great and strong man, lacking in prudence, fell from high to low estate because he fondly loved, and foolishly confided in, a treacherous woman.

Thus during the second period of Christian hermeneutics, writers in and out of the Schools, although they repeated and perpetuated the essential features of the Samson tradition as they had inherited it from the Church Fathers, wrought great changes in the connotations surrounding the name of Samson. Between the eighth and fourteenth centuries literal interpretation persisted, but its prestige was shaken and it leaned more and more towards the circumstantial realism of what has here been termed historical interpretation. Although they had some misgivings about certain aspects of Samson's career, the writers of the most prolific period of medieval exegesis continued to regard Samson as a saint. During this period literal and allegorical interpretation were often drawn together by writers who did not think of them as irreconcilable because they had begun to accept a convention of levels of meaning in Scripture. There are indications that in this period—perhaps as a result of such dissatisfaction as that expressed by Rupert of St. Heribert—the course of allegorical interpretation was, for the first time, diverted in the direction of the moral interpretation, or tropology, later adopted by Renaissance commentators. At the same time the Christian interest in Samson shifted to the tragic aspects of his story: his earlier and more sensational feats were all but forgotten; but his fall, his misery in dark captivity, and his death in the stronghold of his foes—these elements of his story were set forth poignantly in sermon, gloss, hymn, and poem.

Chapter V

THE SAMSON TRADITION IN THE RENAISSANCE

THAT part of hermeneutic literature which pertains to Samson was affected surprisingly little by the great break in the Christian tradition which began at the opening of the sixteenth century when Luther posted his theses in Wittenberg. The Reformation—in spite of the impassable ecclesiastical and doctrinal crevasses which resulted from its schisms—left few traces in interpretation of the Old Testament. This fact is best demonstrated by reference to Renaissance commentaries which are omnium gatherums, drawing together and interweaving great quantities of earlier exegesis to expound a single biblical text. Among the commentaries of this sort are Peter Martyr's *In Librum Iudicum Commentarii Doctissimi* (1571), the glosses in Jean de la Haye's *Biblia Maxima* (1660), Cornelius à Lapide's *Commentarius in Ioshue, Iudicum, et Ruth* (1664), and Matthew Poole's *Synopsis Criticorum* (1669). Although La Haye and Lapide were Roman Catholics and Peter Martyr and Poole were Protestants, there is no significant difference between the kinds of writers to whom they refer as authorities. Both Roman Catholic and Protestant omnium gatherums returned to the early Fathers of the Church in seeking authority, and both parties came away with essentially the same answers to their questions. In his *Calender of Scripture* (London, 1575), William Patten, an Anglican, cited a wide variety of authorities for his commentary on the Book of Judges, among whom were such early Fathers as Augustine, Origen, and Procopius, the Lutheran Johann Brenz, and the Protestant Peter Martyr.[1] Matthew Poole, also an Anglican, was even more promiscuous: in annotating the Samson story alone he referred to Josephus, Jerome, Theodoret, Augustine, Se-

---

[1] Sigs. Ddd i r-Ddd vi r.

rarius, Lapide, Bonfrerius, Torniellus, Salianus, Arias Montanus, Lyra, Tostadus, Peter Martyr, Tirinus, Glasse, Cajetan, and a number of others, mixing Roman Catholic and Protestant without discrimination. Because Renaissance exegetes ranged so widely, and because this is an analytical study of the Samson tradition, not a history of the Christian Church or its theological doctrines, very little attention will be paid here to differences between Catholic and Protestant, or among Protestant sects, unless they happen to affect the Renaissance conception of Samson.

1

THERE were five main trends in biblical exegesis during the fifteenth, sixteenth, and seventeenth centuries. The literal and allegorical methods, which had arisen in the schools of Antioch and Alexandria and persisted throughout the Middle Ages, were still practised in Renaissance commentaries and were still of primary importance. Growing out of literalism, and inseparable from it, was a new rationalistic interpretation, the most significant contribution to Christian hermeneutics during the Renaissance. In addition to allegorical exegesis, and based upon it, were the other two figurative interpretations: tropological, or moral, stemming from Rupert of St. Heribert, and anagogical, or mystical, stemming from the Victorines.

In writings related to Samson during this period there is very little strictly literal interpretation, certainly none comparable to that of Origen or that of the *Chronicon Paschale*. Even commentaries in which literalism predominates over allegory are not infused with that perfect faith in the Word which one can find here and there in writings of the patristic period.[2] Many commentators tried, as had Origen and Au-

---

[2] See, for example, Michaelis Glyca, *Annales* (*Pat. Graec.*, CLVIII, 315-22); Alfonsus Tostadus, *Commentarius in Judicum* (1491), in *Opera* (Venice, 1728), X, 200-68; Martin Luther, *Vorlesung über das Buch der Richter*, ed. Georg Buchwald (Leipzig, 1884), pp. 71-78; Benedictus Arias Montanus, *De Varia Republica: sive, Commentarius in Librum Iudicum* (Antwerp, 1592), pp. 499-580; and Jean de la Haye, *Biblia Maxima* (Paris, 1660), IV, 96-125.

gustine, to sustain the literal sense by means of linguistic exegesis and verbal emendations;[3] but in the Renaissance, as in the period of the Schoolmen, literal interpretation usually took the form of history. In fact, the nearest approach to genuinely literal interpretation is to be found in such historical works as the *Annales* of Michaelis Glyca, the *De Varia Republica* of Arias Montanus, and the *Annales Sacri et Profani* of Augustinus Torniellus.[4] Salianus' commentary on Samson is typical of this group of historical works. In thirty pages of annals covering the period of Samson's life, Salianus placed Samson in his historical context and considered such questions as whether, and in what sense, he was a judge of Israel, and whether he succeeded in liberating his people from the Philistines. Samson's life and death were treated here as events of historio-political significance, and the interpretation is literal inasmuch as the Danite's career is accepted as historical fact. Salianus dated Samson's death 2899 years after the Creation of the World, 1243 years after the Flood, 436 years after the crossing of the Red Sea, 356 years after the giving of the Law, twenty-nine years after the fall of Troy, and 1154 years before the birth of Christ. His account of the story is based on numerous and varied authorities, among whom are Josephus, Origen, Theodoret, Ambrose, Jerome, Paulinus of Nola, Isidore of Seville, Petrus Comestor, Arias Montanus,

---

[3] Luther, *op.cit.*, pp. 71-78; Arias Montanus, *op.cit.*, pp. 499-580; Salomon Glasse on Judges 16, in *Philologia Sacra, qua Totius SS. Veteris et Novi Testamenti Scripturae tum Stylus et Literatura . . . Expenditur* (Frankfurt and Leipzig, 1691); Patten, *op.cit.*, fol. 164ᵛ; Jacobus Tirinus, *Prolegomena in S. Scripturam* (1632), (Venice, 1724), pp. 76ff.

[4] The *Annales* of Salianus were printed at Paris in 1619, 1620, 1621, 1622, 1624, 1635, and 1641, at Strassburg in 1620 and 1638. The *Annales* of Torniellus were printed in a number of places in 1610, 1611, 1620, 1622, 1636, 1639, 1640, 1660, and 1669. See Johann Georg Walch, *Bibliotheca Theologica Selecta Litterariis Adnotationibus Instructa* (Jena, 1757-1765), an excellent source of bibliographical information about Renaissance commentaries. See also Martinus Lipenus, *Bibliotheca Realis Theologica Omnium Materiarum, Rerum et Titulorum, in Universo SS. Theologiae Studio Occurrentium* (Frankfurt am Main, 1685). Du Bartas' treatment of Samson in *La Seconde Sepmaine* ("Les Capitaines," lines 767-96, in *Works*, ed. Holmes, *et al.* [Chapel Hill, 1940], III, 332f.) is purely historical and introduces nothing which could be considered interpretation into the Samson story.

Peter Martyr, Lyra, Cajetan, and Serarius. This history of Samson closes with an epitaph which, supposedly, his kinsmen wrote for his tomb:

Samson heros mille prodigiis inclytus, imo totus ipse prodigium, hoc marmore clausus quiescit. Nam prodigio denunciatur ab angelo, concipitur a sterili matre, et nascitur ad populi libertatem. . . . Prodigio denique columnas ingentes, multorum millium sedem quassat, et concutit; et cum universo Dagonis templo, deiicit, ac devolvit in praeceps, et suis moriens oppressus trophaeis, hostem ac servitutem populi sui eodem sepulchro concludit.[5]

The second main trend—and, in terms of the history of interpretation as a whole, certainly the most significant trend— of biblical exegesis in the Renaissance was the rationalistic interpretation which grew out of literalism. In the Samson tradition this rationalistic criticism seems to have appeared first near the end of the fifteenth century in Alfonsus Tostadus' commentaries on the Heptateuch.[6] Tostadus wrote one of the longest and most detailed of all the commentaries on the story, devoting twenty-one folio pages to Chapter 13 alone. He seems to have been a man who believed in asking the fundamental questions and in thinking out his own answers to them. He wondered whether Samson was consecrated within the womb of his mother or upon emerging from it; why the angel appeared first to the woman rather than to Manoa; whether Samson sinned in taking to wife the Philistine woman of Timnath; how he was able to carry off the gates of Gaza without being intercepted by the guards; why he always loved Philistine women; why the Philistines did not kill him when he lay asleep in Dalila's lap. Tostadus even asked how Samson's kinsmen were able to identify his body in the ruins of the temple. The full answers which he gave

---

[5] *Annales Ecclesiastici Veterus Testamenti* (Strassburg, 1620), II, 441-72. Even here, however, there is allegory mixed with historical interpretation: Salianus devoted two and a half pages (169ff.) to a presentation of all established parallels between Samson and Christ.

[6] *Opera* (Venice, 1728), X, 200-68. According to Walch, *op.cit.*, IV, 449, the earliest edition of these commentaries bears the imprint Hispali, 1491. Subsequent editions appeared in Venice, 1530 and 1596, and in Cologne, 1613.

to all such questions are in common-sense terms; there is no reference to the miraculous, no pietistic reliance on faith. Tostadus honestly attempted to answer honest questions in such a way as to satisfy the reason in the mind of man. This rationalistic exegesis is exemplified, too, in John Marbecke's *A Booke of Notes and Commonplaces* (London, 1581), where the only reference to Samson is found in an article on foxes. Marbecke was concerned about explaining how it had been possible for Samson to catch three hundred foxes:

> If a man aske how *Sampson* get so manie foxes, he must understand, that as there are sundrie Regions, so are there also in them, manie sundrie increase of things. In some place there are manie horses, and those faire: In some place, there is great abundance of cattell: In *England* there is great plentie of Connies, & so is there in the ilands called *Baleares*. In those regions a man maie easelie in one daie, & in a little ground take 3. or 400. Conies, which to some peradventure might seem incredible: And so it is said, y^t ther is a verie great abundance of Foxes in *Siria*, & speciallie in ye borders of *Iewrie*. . . . And *Sampson* tooke them either by his owne industrie, or by the helpe of his friends.[7]

Likewise, in Arias Montanus' *De Varia Republica* (Antwerp, 1592), in Sebastian Schmidt's *In Librum Iudicum Commentarius* (Strassburg, 1684), and in Bishop Simon Patrick's *Commentary upon the Books of Joshua, Judges, and Ruth* (London, 1702), one finds this form of rationalistic interpretation, this incipient "higher criticism" occupying an increasingly important place. Bishop Patrick's discussion of Samson's fox-catching is characteristic of this strain in Renaissance biblical exegesis as it passed over into the temper of the Enlightenment:

> Some make a difficulty to believe this, because Foxes are subtil Creatures, and not easily caught. But they should consider such things as these. . . . That this Country abounded with Foxes, from whence several places had their names, particularly one in the Tribe of *Dan* . . . , and that under this name of Foxes, may be comprehended a Creature very like a Fox, called *Thoes*, which go together in Herds; so that two Hundred (as good Authors report)

[7] P. 420f.

have been seen in a company together. And next, a Day and a Night: but there might be a Week, or a Months time allowed for the accomplishment of his design. In which his Servants, and Neighbours, and Friends, no doubt, assisted him, if he desired it. So that such a number might be caught, in a short time. For they were not caught, as some imagin, only by Hunting; but in Snares and Nets.[8]

As this explanation reveals, Bishop Patrick was not a religious man by old standards. He did his best to make Samson's story probable in human terms, to make it acceptable to the reason. He was not one to shrug his shoulders and say, "But it was a miracle." He felt the want of an explanation, and his explanation really implies skepticism in its every line, no matter how often he might insist that there should be "no doubt."

The path of literalism was always stony and steep. The writers who followed it always turned aside into emendation, or philology, or history, or, as has been shown, into rationalistic apologetics. The way of allegory, the third of the five main trends in Renaissance interpretation of Scripture, was straight and smooth, as it had been for centuries. The allegorical interpretation of Samson is found in numerous writings in the fifteenth, sixteenth, and seventeenth centuries: in the glosses of Nicholas de Lyra's *Biblia Sacra*, in a sermon by Archbishop Sandys (1519-1588), in James Calfhill's *Answer to John Martiall* (1565), in Henoch Clapham's *Briefe of the Bible* (1596), in Joseph Hall's *Contemplations* (1615), in George Herbert's *The Temple* (1633), in John Donne's *Biathanatos* (1644), in the *Genealogia Christi* (1657), and in John Diodati's *Pious and Learned Annotations* (1664).[9] There are de-

---

[8] P. 540f. The woodcuts in Arias Montanus' *De Varia Republica* graphically exemplify the spirit of rationalism in Renaissance biblical criticism. See Plates I and II. Many commentators were hard put to it to explain how Samson had been able to carry off the city gates, and they also found it difficult to account for the destruction of the Temple of Dagon. Plate I shows Samson bearing away the gates of Gaza on his shoulders, and the floor-plan in Plate II is designed to prove that a temple roof could be supported by two main columns located in such a way as to admit of the ruin of the whole building if they were pushed down.

[9] Lyra, *Biblia Sacra cum Glossis* (London, 1545), II, fol. 51ʳ; Edwin Sandys, *Sermons*, ed. John Ayre (Cambridge, 1841), p. 370f.; Calfhill,

I. Samson Carrying the Gates of Gaza

Benedictus Arias Montanus, *De Varia Republica*, Antwerp, 1592,
p. 549 (Union Theological Seminary Library)

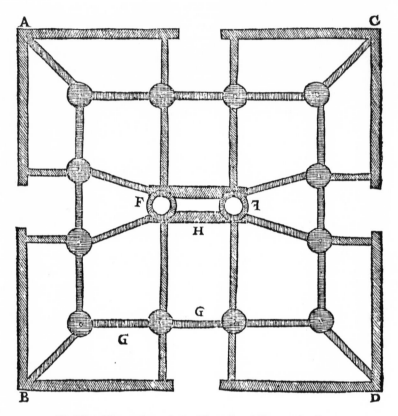

II. The Floor-plan of the Temple of Dagon in Gaza
Benedictus Arias Montanus, *De Varia Republica*, Antwerp, 1592,
p. 571 (Union Theological Seminary Library)

Wherein Sampſon *reſembled* Chriſt.

Ampſons *birth was foretold by an Angel, and was wonderfull, in regard that his mother had bin barren, and God gave her ſtrength to conceive and bear him.*

Jeſus *his birth was foretold by the Angel* Gabriel, *and was miraculous in regard that his mother knew not any man, and that the Holy Ghoſt gave her ſtrength to conceive and bring him forth.*

Sampſon *came into the world when the Iſraelits were much oppreſſed by* their enemies the Philiſtines, *and freed them from that heavy yoak and miſery.*

Chriſt *came into the world when* Satan *the Prince of the World bragd, that all the Kingdoms of the world were his : and then* Chriſt *ſpiritually delivered us from the tyranny of him and his Angels.*

Sampſon *aſſiſted by the ſpirit of God comming upon him, tore a Lion in peeces, as on would have rent a kid.*

Chriſt *being of almighty power as he is God, eaſily overcame & confounded* Satan, *who is like a roaring Lion , ſeeking whom he may devoure.*

The Philiſtines *had ever miſcheivous minds and plots againſt* Sampſon, *but could not effect their deſignes untill the Spirit of God ſuſpended it ſelfe, and permitted their malice to ſhew it ſelf.*

Chriſts *enemies often deviſed and praſtiſed to doe him miſcheif: but could doe nothing , untill* Chriſts *Deity ſuſpended its power, and permitted them to exerciſe their cruelty.*

Sampſon *gathered no armie of warriours to aſſiſt him in his conqueſts , but himſelfe alone by the aſſiſtance of the Spirit of God performed them.*

Jeſus *had none of all the people with him in his conqueſt.* Eſ. 63. *Himſelf alone by his divine power obtained the victory over our enemies.*

Dalila *with kiſſes pretending love, for bribes betrayed* Sampſon *into the hands of them who ſought his life.*

Judas *with a kind ſalute and kiſſe made a ſhew of honouring* Jeſus, *but for a bribe betrayed him into the power of his enemies.*

V   Sampſon

III. Tabular Representation of Allegorical Parallels
between Christ and Samson
Thomas Hayne, *The General View of the Holy Scriptures*, London,
1640, p. 217f (Princeton Theological Seminary Library)

Sampſon was taken and willingly bound by the Iſraelites his own people, who would not kill him: and then was delivered to the Philiſtines ; but the cords which bound him, could not hold him.

Chriſt was taken and willingly bound by the Jews his own people, who could not put him to death. The Romans had taken that power from them. Then the Jews delivered him to the Romans; But neither thoſe bonds, nor the bonds of death Pſa. 116. could hold him. Act. 2. 24.

The Philiſtines having Sampſon in Azza a ſtrong Citie, ſhut the gates upon him, thought there to hold him faſt, and to prevail over him ; but hee carried away the gates of the Citie, and fruſtrated their plot.

The Jews, and Romans having Chriſt in his grave a ſtrong priſon houſe, had him ſhut up with a grave ſtone ſealed, and kept with a watch, and thought there to hold him faſt : but he conquered death and the grave, and roſe again to life, never to die more.

The ſpirit of God, which ſtrengthened Sampſon, permitting, he was bound, led away, mocked, had his eyes bored out, and died willingly, that the Philiſtines might not exerciſe their crueltie upon him: and at his death kild more by pulling down the houſe on the Philiſtines, than in his life time.

Chriſts Divinitie permitting it, he was bound, led to the Judgement hall, mocked, had his feet and hands pierced, willingly yeelded up his ſpirit, and prevented their crueltie, who would have broken his legs : made the Jews houſe deſolate, and left them to diverſe and moſt miſerable deaths, and the Romans to continual bloodſhed in the Emperors Wars.

2869. *From the account in* Abdons *time to the death of* Sampſon *in this year are* 20 *years.*

Eli

IV. Tabular Representation of Allegorical Parallels between Christ and Samson

tailed summaries of the allegory which had accumulated about
Samson since the time of Ambrose in Jean de la Haye's *Biblia
Maxima*, in Jacobus Tirinus' *Commentarius in S. Scripturam*,
and in Jacobus Bonfrerius' *Commentarii in Ioshuam, Iudices,
et Ruth*; but Thomas Hayne's *General View of the Holy
Scriptures* (1640) contains a complete tabular analysis of the
aspects "wherein Sampson resembled Christ," which reveals
with unmistakable clarity the enduring vitality of the allegorical tradition.[10] Most of the ancient parallels were still valid
in the seventeenth century, and Hayne presented them all
with a few new figures. "*Sampsons* birth was foretold by an
Angel, and was wonderfull, in regard that his mother had
bin barren, and God gave her strength to conceive and bear
him"; "*Jesus* his birth was foretold by the Angel *Gabriel*,
and was miraculous in regard that his mother knew not any
man, and that the Holy Ghost gave her strength to conceive
and bring her forth." "*Sampson* assisted by the spirit of God
comming upon him, tore a Lion in peeces, as on[e] would
have rent a kid"; "*Christ* being of almighty power as he is
God, easily overcame & confounded Satan, who is like a roaring Lion, seeking whom he may devoure." "*Dalila* with
kisses pretending love, for bribes betrayed *Sampson* into the
hands of them who sought his life"; "*Judas* with a kind salute
and kisse made a shew of honouring *Jesus*, but for a bribe
betrayed him into the power of his enemies." "The spirit
of God, which strengthened *Sampson*, permitting, he was
bound, led away, mocked, had his eyes bored out, and died
willingly"; "*Christs* Divinitie permitting it, he was bound,
led to the Judgement hall, mocked, had his feet and hands
pierced, willingly yeelded up his spirit."

Answer, ed. Richard Gibbings (Cambridge, 1846), p. 336; Clapham,
Briefe of the Bible (Edinburgh, 1596), p. 68f.; Hall, *Contemplations*
(London, 1615), III, 185-280; Herbert, "Sunday," lines 43-9, in *Works*,
ed. F. E. Hutchinson (Oxford, 1941), p. 76; Donne, *Biathanatos*, III, V,
4 (London, 1644), pp. 199ff.; *Genealogia Christi* (London, 1657), quoted
in Todd, ed., *Works of Milton* (London, 1809), V, 348; Diodati, *Annotations*, 4th ed. (London, 1664), Judges 16:3.
[10] P. 217f. See Plates III and IV.

Such a bond existed between the story of Samson and the story of Christ in Milton's own period that it is impossible to suppose that Milton himself could have been unaware of the larger implications of his tragedy.

The fourth main trend of biblical exegesis in the Renaissance was tropological, or moral, interpretation. The exploiting of this form of exegesis seems to have been one of the few hermeneutic results of the Reformation. The more Luther and his successors did to free the individual believer from the authority of the priest, the more they subjected him to the authority of the Bible. Before the Reformation, the priest had been every Christian's means of access to knowledge of the will of God, every Christian's moral guide; after the Reformation, for Protestant Christians, the priest was deposed, and the Bible became man's key to the will of God, man's storehouse of moral guidance. This change resulted, for a time, in an even greater concern with problems of scriptural interpretation; and it may also have been for this reason that Luther revived the tropological interpretation which had been practised in the twelfth century by Rupert of St. Heribert. In Luther's view Samson was a negative exemplum, an object lesson teaching us by his killing and his lechery not to do likewise.[11] Tropological exegesis was continued by Johann Brenz, a follower of Luther's, whose *In Librum Iudicum et Ruth* was printed at The Hague in 1535. Brenz interpreted Samson as "exemplum prudentiae," and "exemplum obedientiae et reverentiae." He took Samson's slaying the lion as a symbol of the victory over Satan which all true believers can achieve.[12] In a series of nineteen sermons in his *Commentary upon the Whole Book of Judges* (London, 1615), Richard Rogers developed the moral interpretation of Samson as fully as might be thought possible, wringing from each verse of Scripture its total homiletic usefulness:

[11] *Vorlesung über das Buch der Richter*, ed. Georg Buchwald (Leipzig, 1884), pp. 71-78.
[12] Pp. 198-201.

The Lord doth raise a deliuerer out of the tribe of *Dan* . . . this tribe being one of the meanest: It teacheth that God will serue himself by the meaner sort as well as by the mightier and greater, when it pleaseth him.[13]

Samson, as a Nazarite, was forbidden to cut his hair. This rule signifies to us "that much time should not be taken vp in too nicely trimming and looking to our bodies" (p. 616). Rogers himself stated clearly the assumption which led to the practice of tropological interpretation, and it is an assumption which reveals much of the whole religious temper of his age:

Indeed God doe not now, as in times past, I meane, he dealeth not the same way that he did with *Samson* and many other then. For in those daies he spake to our fathers. and inlightened them after sundrie manners, but in these latter times, the outward meane that he useth, is chiefly his word truly preached. . . . We looke not for reuelations, nor Angels ministerie now.[14]

In this survey of the general characteristics of biblical criticism in the Renaissance, only anagogical interpretation remains to be considered. Commentators who adopted this form of exposition found in Scripture a mystical symbolism expressive of large ultimate truths about God and God's ways towards Man. In his *Commentarius in Ioshue, Iudicum, et Ruth*, Cornelius à Lapide clearly distinguished among literal, allegorical, tropological, and anagogical senses of Scripture. For example, he gave all four levels of meaning in a discussion of the significance of Samson's strength and its residing in his hair. In the literal sense this feature of the story means that the strength of any Nazarite lies in his faithfulness to his vows, of which his unshorn locks are a badge; in the allegorical sense, Samson herein was a figure of Christ, who is our head; in the tropological sense, the hair of Samson denotes the cogitations and intentions of Man, sound thoughts spring-

[13] P. 614. Rogers' comment on Samson is in Sermons 71-89, pp. 611-790.
[14] P. 655. Roman Catholic commentators had excellent ancient authority, too, for the practice of tropological exegesis, and many examples of this interpretation can be found in representative Catholic commentaries. See Lyra, *Biblia Sacra* (London, 1545), II, fols. 51ʳ and 52ʳ; La Haye, *Biblia Maxima* (Paris, 1660), IV, 96-125, where the comments of Lyra, Estius, Menochius, and Tirinus are reproduced.

ing from a sound mind; and, finally, in the anagogical sense, the hair signified that Samson's strength was supernatural, a special gift of God, and it kept him mindful that such special endowments were his only so long as he was free from sin.[15] Sebastian Schmidt made it plain that Samson's strength did not reside in his hair, that the cutting of his hair did not make him weak; the hair was, however, a symbol of his falling away from virtue—he had sinned, and he lost his strength for that reason, not merely because his hair was cut.[16]

2

THE presence of these four basic and divergent ways of interpreting the story of Samson and the rise of rationalistic criticism made him a very complex concept in the mind of the Renaissance. By the beginning of the seventeenth century Samson meant a bewildering variety of things. This variety must now be ordered and displayed for the purpose of defining, as clearly as possible, the conceptions of Samson which could have existed in the minds of the first readers of *Samson Agonistes*.

In nearly all the secular literature of England during the sixteenth and seventeenth centuries, Samson was treated exactly as he had been treated during the medieval period in the *Cursor Mundi*, *The Monk's Tale*, the *Confessio Amantis*, and the *Fall of Princes*. The poets of the Renaissance, almost without exception, adopted the medieval literary conception of Samson as a great man brought low by a woman's treachery. In Shakespeare's *Love's Labour's Lost* (I, ii), for example, where Armado confesses that he is in love and begs Moth to comfort him by telling of famous lovers, Samson is mentioned, along with Hercules, as one "of good repute and carriage" who was in love. After Moth has spoken of Samson's misfortunes, Armado concludes: "There is no evil angel but Love. Yet was Samson so tempted, and he had an excellent strength. Yet was Salomon so seduced, and he had a very good wit."

[15] P. 175.
[16] *In Librum Judicum Commentarius* (Strassburg, 1684), p. 1315f.

George Gascoigne, too, arguing in *The Droome of Doomes Day* (1576) that "wyne and women have caused many wyse men to fall from the faythe," remembered that love of woman had "seduced *Sampson*, and perverted *Salomon*." And in the *Anatomy of Melancholy* (1621) Burton maintained that "Samson's strength was enervated by lust," and he named Samson in company with David, Solomon, Hercules, and Socrates—all examples of "the most staid, discreet, grave, generous, and wise," who, when "overtaken with this passion," "commit many absurdities, many indecorums, unbefitting their gravity and persons."[17] The same version of Samson's story is echoed by Spenser in *The Faerie Queene* (V, viii, 2), where, by way of warning his readers of the dangers and the power of passion, the poet cited Samson—exactly as the earliest Fathers of the Church had done—as an *a fortiori* example:

> So whylome learnd that mighty Iewish swaine,
> Each of whose lockes did match a man in might,
> To lay his spoiles before his lemans traine. . . .
> Such wondrous powre hath wemens faire aspect,
> To captiue men, and make them all the world reiect.[18]

Such use of Samson as an exemplum was felt to be pointedly

[17] Gascoigne, *Works*, ed. J. W. Cunliffe (Cambridge, 1910), II, 248; Burton, *Anatomy of Melancholy*, ed. A. R. Shilleto (London, 1893), III, 60, 176, 237. In these two Renaissance references to Samson there is a reflection of another feature of the medieval conception of Samson. Before the end of the Middle Ages Samson's name had found a place in one of those rhetorical proverb-formulas with which many spoken and written preachments were garnished. G. R. Owst (*Literature and the Pulpit in Medieval England* [Cambridge, 1933], p. 385) cites this formula as one of the favorite sayings of the homilists: "Who was strenger than Sampson, wyser than Salomon, holyer than David? And ȝit they were al overcomen by the queryntise and whiles of women" (MS. Harl. 45, fol. 101f.). Owst lists many repetitions of the tag (*op.cit.*, p. 385, note 2), and I have found it also in Chaucer's *Parson's Tale* (lines 953ff.), in *The Conception of Mary*, lines 162f. (*Ludus Coventriae*, ed. K. S. Bloch, *EETS*, extra series, no. 120 [London, 1922], p. 68), in John Lyly's *Euphues: the Anatomy of Wit*, ed. R. W. Bond (Oxford, 1902), I, 308f., and in William Caxton's *Mirrour of the World*, ed. O. H. Prior, *EETS*, extra series, no. 110 (London, 1913), p. 154.
[18] See also Phineas Fletcher, *The Apollyonists*, IV, xxiii, in *Works*, ed. F. S. Boas (Cambridge, 1908), I, 169, and Francis Quarles, *Historie of Samson*, Meditation 19, in *Works*, ed. A. B. Grosart (Edinburgh, 1880-81), II, 162.

effective because he was still thought of as an exceptionally gifted agent of God, endowed with superhuman strength by virtue of the indwelling of the Holy Spirit.[19] Moreover, Samson was still regarded as a saint. Not even the popular secular notion of Samson as a ruined lover affected this ancient conception. To be sure, Calvin admitted that Samson, "overcome by the blandishments of a concubine," had "inconsiderately betrayed the safety of the whole people." Nevertheless, Calvin argued, "in all the saints something reprehensible is ever to be found," and they are, notwithstanding, "approved by God" because of their faith.[20] Along with this conviction that Samson was a saint went a desire to absolve him from whatever faults he had been charged with. John Marbecke, for example, altered the biblical account by saying that Samson "got him to the Citie of Gaza, and lodged in a womans house that solde vittayles," in spite of the fact that the Bible represented him as going in unto a harlot (Judges 16:1).[21]

The fact that Samson had brought about his own death, however, still made trouble for the commentators who ac-

---

[19] Calvin, for example, in commenting on Hebrews 11, defended Samson and the others named there, saying that "they all followed the guidance of God, and being animated by his promise, undertook what was commanded them being honoured with the testimony of the Holy Spirit" (*Commentaries on the Epistle of Paul the Apostle to the Hebrews*, trans. John Owen [Edinburgh, 1853], p. 302f.). Johann Brenz (*In Librum Iudicum et Ruth Commentarius* [The Hague, 1535], p. 204) explained that Samson was justified in killing Philistines because he had a vocation from God. The same view of Samson as God's agent granted supernatural strength to serve God's cause can be found in the following: Cajetan, *Opera* (London, 1637), II, 62; Lyra, *Biblia Sacra* (London, 1545), II, fol. 52ʳ; "Breeches" (or "Geneva") Bible (London, 1599), p. 88; Henry Bullinger, *Decades*, trans. H. I., ed. Thomas Harding (Cambridge, 1850), III, 209f.; David Pareus, *Opera Theologica* (Frankfurt, 1647), I, 490-93; Thomas Hayne, *The General View of the Holy Scriptures* (London, 1640), p. 215; Joseph Hall, *A Plaine and Familiar Explication* (London, 1633), p. 99f.

[20] *Op.cit.*, p. 303. See also Edward Hutchins, *Sampsons Iawbone against the Spiritual Philistine* (London, 1601), sig. Aᵛ; Thomas Hayne, *General View*, p. 216; John Donne, *Biathanatos* (London, 1644), p. 199.

[21] *The Lyues of Holy Sainctes* (London, 1574), p. 72. In his *Synopsis Antiquitatum Hebraicarum* (Oxford, 1616), p. 154, Thomas Godwin classified Samson as the highest sort of Nazarite since he was a "perpetual" Nazarite, rather than a "temporary" Nazarite, and since he was "chosen" in the womb by God.

cepted him as a saint. Some of them, like Cajetan,[22] still excused Samson from suicide, arguing that his self-destruction was indirect and concomitant with his pursuing Jehovah's cause against the enemies of the Israelites. But Donne took a stand against this reasoning and declared that Samson intended his own death because he prayed to God saying "Let me die with the Philistines." Nevertheless, in harmony with the whole argument of *Biathanatos*, Donne maintained that Samson's suicide was manifestly justified by the fact that God gave him strength for that purpose and by the fact that he had "the same reason to kill himselfe, which hee had to kill them, and the same authoritie, and the same priviledge, and safeguard from sinne," so that he "dyed . . . with the same zeal as Christ."[23] John Lightfoot, on the contrary, believed that, although Samson "had done great acts," in the end he "came off with some foul blot," for he "pulled down the house upon his own head, and so became 'felo-de-se,' or guilty of his own death."[24] Indeed, Cornelius à Lapide had even given it as his opinion that Samson was not really a martyr at all because he fought and destroyed himself, while martyrs suffer rather than fight and are destroyed in consequence of their patience.[25]

The commentators of the Renaissance were generally agreed that Samson, though a saint, had fallen into sin. In fact, one writer believed that the entire Book of Judges serves "to shew the iudgement of God against obstinat sinners."[26] David Pareus, Thomas Hayne, Henry Bullinger, Joseph Hall, and Sebastian Schmidt all made it clear that Samson lost his strength, not because his hair was cut, but because he had sinned by failing in his Nazaritic vows, in consorting with

---

[22] *Opera* (London, 1637), II, 63. See also Sebastian Schmidt, *In Librum Judicum Commentarius*, p. 1318f.

[23] P. 201.

[24] "A Sermon Preached upon Judges 11:39," in *Whole Works*, ed. J. R. Pitman (London, 1822-1825), VIII, 151.

[25] *Commentarius in Ioshue, Iudicum, Ruth* (Antwerp, 1664), p. 178, col. 1. Cf. *Samson Agonistes*, lines 1287-88, and below p. 98, n. 23.

[26] Edward Vaughan, *Ten Introductions How to Read all the Books in the Holy Bible* (London, 1594), sig. F4ᵛ.

harlots, and in betraying God's secret to Dalila.[27] Bullinger, for example, after defining the status, vows, and duties of Nazariteship, added:

By all this we may plainly perceive what and how great the sin of Samson was, who was a Nazarite to the Lord. For because he did not only lurk in the brothel-house with the harlot, but did also bewray the secret of God . . . , and cast behind him the covenant made with God, whereof his hair was a sure testimony; therefore did the Lord forsake him, and that wonderful strength which he had from heaven was clean taken from him.

In Renaissance commentaries, as in Renaissance poetry, Samson's fall was blamed on "his immoderate affections toward a wicked woman,"[28] and thus again attention was called to Dalila, and emphasis was placed upon her part in Samson's ruin. Allegorically, she was interpreted as a figure of Judas, and her attempts to learn from Samson the secret of his strength were compared also with Satan's temptation of Christ. But the question most often discussed in the Renaissance was whether Dalila had been Samson's wife or his concubine. Some of the commentators followed Chrysostom, Cassianus, Sulpicius Severus, and Pererius in thinking that she was Samson's wife;[29] but Bonfrerius and most others agreed with Josephus, Ambrose, Jerome, Montanus, and Serarius that Dalila was Samson's concubine, and Bullinger even identified her with the harlot of Gaza.[30] Cajetan seems to have been the only writer who made any attempt to defend Dalila. To begin with, he believed that she was "Hebraea," not "Pelistina";

[27] Pareus, *Opera Theologica* (Frankfurt, 1647), I, 490-93; Hayne, *General View*, p. 216; Bullinger, *Decades*, III, vi (ed. Harding, III, 209); Hall, *Contemplations* (London, 1615), III, 259-62; Schmidt, *In Librum Judicum*, p. 1315f. See also William Prynne, *Histrio-mastix* (London, 1633), p. 229f.

[28] "Breeches" Bible, *in loc.* Judges 16:17. See also Marbecke, *Lyues of Holy Sainctes*, p. 71: "Finallye, thorowe his inordinate affection to Dalila his wyfe, he lost Goddes excellent gift"; and Hall, *Contemplations*, III, 259.

[29] See Tirinus, *Prolegomena in S. Scripturam* (Venice, 1724), p. 77, col. 2; La Haye, *Biblia Maxima*, IV, 118; Salianus, *Annales*, II, 441-72; Lapide, *Commentarius*, p. 174, col. 1; Marbecke, *Lyues*, p. 71f.

[30] La Haye, *op.cit.*, IV, 118; Bonfrerius, *Commentarii in Ioshuam, Iudices, et Ruth* (Paris, 1631), p. 368, col. 2; Bullinger, *op.cit.*, III, 209.

and he suggested also that the Philistines broke faith with her, that she had not bargained for so much cruelty as they ultimately inflicted upon Samson.[31]

Whether they believed Dalila to be Samson's wife or his concubine, all the writers who expounded the story during this period were agreed that he sinned and fell and that his love for Dalila was the cause of this fall. These ideas were often repeated and never debated. Neither did any Renaissance writer question whether, having fallen, Samson repented his sins. Nicholas de Lyra argued that the fact that his wonderful locks grew long again during his captivity signifies that any sinner, no matter how deeply fallen into evil, will be restored to grace if he repents. Henry Bullinger said that Samson "repented heartily, and called upon the name of the Lord: whereby it came to pass, that, when his hair grew forth again, his strength returned." According to Bishop Hall, "his haire grew together with his repentance." Richard Rogers, too, thought of Samson as penitent:

Samson sitting in the irksome prison in paine of body, but greater of mind, did think of his euil course, and frō what estate he was falne, and what miserie he was in, and repented for it, after due consideration.

It was Salianus' opinion that Samson repented his sins and "divinam clementiam implorat." Sebastian Schmidt thought there could be no doubt about it at all and referred his reader to Serarius, who had thought of Samson as "de cordis sui profundo ad Deum clamans, lachrymas fundens." And Bishop Patrick believed that Samson "repented, no doubt, of his folly" and that he continued for some time "in this state of penitence."[32]

As the result of allegorical interpretation, of course, Samson was still regarded as a type of Christ, and all the events of

[31] *Opera* (London, 1637), II, 62f.
[32] Lyra, *Biblia Sacra*, fol. 51ʳ; Bullinger, *Decades*, III, 209; Hall, *Contemplations*, III, 271ff.; Rogers, *Commentary*, p. 769; Salianus, *Annales*, II, 467, col. 1; Schmidt, *Commentarius*, p. 1316f.; Patrick, *Commentary*, p. 561; cf. also "Breeches" Bible, *in loc.* Judges 16:22, and Pareus, *Opera*, I, 493.

his life had acquired widening circles of connotations which related his story very closely to the life of Christ.[33] Samson was also thought of as an historical personage and a political figure of great importance in the history of Israel. Most commentators referred to him as a ruler of Israel.[34] Moreover, throughout the sixteenth and seventeenth centuries, as in the Middle Ages, writers thought of Samson as the counterpart of Hercules and associated the two in their minds so regularly that they seldom named one without being reminded of the other. From Chaucer, through Gower, Lydgate, and Spenser, to Shakespeare, the two names were coupled in poetry. And in the biblical exegesis of the period the relationship between Samson and Hercules was frequently discussed. Most of the commentators followed Serarius in this matter, saying that he had proved Augustine's supposition that the Greeks had got their Hercules from the Samson of the Jews.[35] In his *Biathanatos* Donne spoke of Samson as "a man so exemplar" that he was long anticipated by the prophets, remembered figuratively in Christ, and copied in his own time by the Greeks in Hercules. And Bishop Patrick deliberately concluded:

It is a very probable conjecture of some great Men, that hence the *Greeks* framed the Fable of their *Hercules*: who lived about his time, and whose name is the same with *Samson's*, if it be derived from *Schemish* the Sun. For *Hercules* is as much as *Orchol*, that which enlightens all, *i.e.* the Sun.[36]

When Milton wrote *Samson Agonistes* he might have expected his readers to have all, or most, of these conceptions in their minds. For during Milton's own lifetime Samson was remembered by many as a tragic lover; as a man of prodigious strength; as the ruler and liberator of Israel; as a great historical personage whose downfall was caused by the treachery

[33] See above p. 68f. and notes 9 and 10.
[34] See above p. 65f.
[35] E.g., Bonfrerius, *Commentarii in Ioshuam, Iudices, et Ruth*, pp. 375ff.; Poole, *Synopsis*, I, *in loc.* Judges 16:30; Tirinus, *Prolegomena*, p. 78, col. I.
[36] *Op.cit.*, p. 567.

of a woman, and therefore as an example of the perils of passion; as a sinner who repented and was restored to grace; as the original of Hercules; as a consecrated Nazarite; as a saint resplendent in unfailing faith; as an agent of God sustained by the Holy Spirit; and as a figure of Christ.

Chapter VI

MILTON'S SAMSON AND THE TRADITION

Such a reconstruction of tradition as has been attempted in the three preceding chapters does not solve all the problems encountered by the modern critic of *Samson Agonistes*. Perhaps its greatest value consists in a general enhancement of the meaning of the poem, in an enrichment afforded by connotations reclaimed from an ever-encroaching sea of oblivion. Neither historical criticism nor any other sort of criticism can ever "explain away" the inscrutable creative imagination of a poet of Milton's greatness. But there are many things in his *Samson Agonistes* which hold more meaning and yield a truer, deeper pleasure to the reader who is mindful of, and acquainted with, the tradition which has been sketched here. The application of much of this connotation to the poem itself must be left to the perception of that reader.

Nevertheless, there are a number of specific applications of this tradition to the poem which remain to be made; there is some additional evidence to be presented; and there are some major conclusions to be stated. It is the purpose of this final chapter to apply the tradition to the poem, to present the rest of the evidence, and to state the critical conclusions which seem to be inescapable. Since the content of this final chapter rests upon the principal critical problems already defined in the introductory chapter, it would be desirable to deal with those problems at last in the same order as was adopted for introducing them at the outset. However, the order which seemed most suitable for the first chapter must be considerably altered in this, for it seems better to destroy the superficial unity and symmetry of the composition than to do violence to the matter. In this chapter, therefore, the following topics will be dealt with in this order: (1) the inconclu-

siveness of previous studies of sources and of the relationship
of *Samson Agonistes* to Greek tragedy, and hence of our established conception of the exact extent and nature of Milton's
originality; (2) Milton's reasons for choosing Samson as a
tragic hero; (3) the specific relation of Milton's treatment
of the Samson story to some of the principal elements of the
tradition; (4) the meaning of *Samson Agonistes* approached
through its title and the concept of the *agon* of life to which
the title is a clue; (5) the meaning of *Samson Agonistes* in
the light of the allegorical interpretation of Samson; (6) the
problem of dramatic structure and of the functions of the
other characters; and (7) a critical hypothesis about the cycli-
cal unity of Milton's three major poems.

1

THE extent and the complexity of the Samson tradition serve
to persuade the Milton critic of the futility and meaningless-
ness of such piecemeal and fragmentary studies of sources as
were reviewed in the opening chapter of this book. Seizing
upon Josephus, or Vondel, or the Book of Job as the source,
or even as a principal source, of Milton's treatment of the
Samson story is, in the light of this immense mass of Samson
literature, as pointless as trying to find the very grain of sand
which held Blake's world. If one claimed as a source for *Samson Agonistes* every text antecedent to Milton's tragedy which
was accessible to Milton and for which some argument of
similarity could be made, then nearly every document here
dealt with might be regarded as a source for the poem. Even
the view that the principal source of *Samson Agonistes* is the
Book of Judges must be more sharply focused to allow for the
intervention of a cloud of tradition between any seventeenth-
century reader and the skeletal story told in those brief chapters of the Old Testament.

The same must be said of all previous efforts to define the
nature of Milton's indebtedness to Greek drama in *Samson
Agonistes*. Even Professor Parker's judicious study of this
problem leaves us with a conception of Milton's originality

which demands some revision. In concluding that, in spite of numerous specific debts to the *Oedipus Coloneus* of Sophocles, *Samson Agonistes* is more than just an imitation of Greek tragedy, Professor Parker left undetermined just what that *more* signifies. And when one has explored the region which encloses all of *Samson Agonistes* not related to Greek tragedy, one returns to the poem convinced that only in *form* are the bonds of similarity significant; the content of *Samson Agonistes*, insofar as it can be distinguished at all from form, has much stronger bonds with regions in which Greek tragedy is a mere pin-point on the map.

However, Jebb's contrary conception of the preponderance of Hebraism in *Samson Agonistes* must also be modified; for, although much of the Samson tradition descends to the seventeenth century in the stream of Judaeo-Christian culture, much also is derived from Graeco-Roman culture as well, as will be more clearly shown in the fourth section of this chapter. Anticipating the conclusion of that section, this much may be said: even one who has followed the course of the Christian tradition as it relates to Milton's Samson must grant that the balance of Judaeo-Christian and Graeco-Roman elements is too delicate to be snatched by a sudden grasp of opinionated generalization.

2

THE history of the Christian conception of Samson helps to explain why, from the time when he first made plans to write a tragedy, Milton perceived a tragic hero in the Samson who seems to be just a tribal hero. Even if one allows that Milton was a more sensitive and imaginative reader of the Book of Judges than are most of us today, one does not thereby explain fully the differences between Milton's Samson and the Samson whom we usually see in Judges. Milton and his contemporaries looked upon Samson in a light which revealed levels of meaning which we have completely forgotten. Samson was a much larger and more significant figure in the late Renaissance than he is today. But the reason why Milton accepted

Samson as a suitable tragic hero can now be made even more specific. As has been shown in the preceding chapters, the Samson tradition had developed in such a way that this Danite's earlier and more purely sensational feats were subordinated and the last part of his life was given ever greater emphasis. This development meant that attention was drawn away from the boastful brawler of the firebrands and the jawbone and directed towards the blind and enervated prisoner of Jehovah's enemies.[1] Josephus long before had suggested that Samson's fall was brought about by *hybris*, and Gregory the Great saw in Samson the exemplification of "mentis caecitas," or *hamartia*. Calvin, too, had perceived in Samson, as in all the most saintly, a "something reprehensible," a flaw for which their faith alone compensated—or, as Milton himself expressed it, "The holiness of the saints is nevertheless imperfect in this life."[2]

In Milton's own period others had written poignantly of the tragic features of the last part of Samson's life. Bishop Hall, Milton's old antagonist, devoted three of his contemplations to Samson and laid great stress on the helplessness of the blind prisoner in Gaza.

As hee passed the street, euery boy of the Philistims could throw stones at him, euery woman could laugh, and shout at him; and what one Philistim doth not say, whiles he lashes him vnto bloud, There is for my brother, or my kinsman, whom thou slewest. . . . This great hart could not but haue broken with indignation, if it had not pacified it selfe with the conscience of the iust desert of all this vengeance. . . . The losse of his eyes showes him his sin; neither could hee see how ill hee had done, till hee saw not. Euen yet, still the God of mercy lookt vpon the blindness of *Sampson*, and in these fetters enlargeth his heart from the worse prison of his sinne. . . . Gods merciful humiliations of his own, are sometimes so seuere, that they seem to differ little from desertions; yet

[1] The tragic aspects of Samson's later career are stressed in Brenz, *In Librum Iudicum et Ruth Commentarius* (The Hague, 1535), pp. 224-30; Richard Rogers, *A Commentary upon the Whole Booke of Judges* (London, 1615), pp. 736-90; Hall, *Contemplations* (London, 1615), III, 259-80; Salianus, *Annales* (Cologne, 1620), II, 465-72.

[2] *De Doctrina Christiana*, I, xxi (Columbia edition, XVI, 14f.).

at the worst, he loues vs bleeding: & when we haue smarted
enough, wee shall feele it.[3]

But in the *Annales* (1620) of Salianus the end of Samson's
story is explicitly designated as tragedy. In a detailed analysis
of the story of Samson, Salianus spoke of Samson's realiza-
tion, upon awaking in the arms of Dalila, that he was bereft
of his divine strength, as the "peripetia luctuosae tragoediae,"
the reversal of sorrowful tragedy, occurring in the fourth act
of Samson's play upon the stage of life. Then he added:
"Nam quintus catastrophem, mortemque Samsonis continet."
Salianus even pointed out that the misery to which Samson
fell was out of proportion to his sin, more grievous than the
fault—the situation calculated by Aristotle (*Poetics*, 13) to
be especially productive of tragic pity.[4]

Furthermore, in Milton's period the conception of the
precise nature of Samson's tragedy had changed in some details. It was no longer thought of only as a *casus viri illustris*
caused by a woman's treachery—as it had been in what has
been revealed here as the typical poetic treatment of the story
in the Middle Ages and the earlier Renaissance; instead it
had come to be regarded more often as a tragedy of failure
in high calling, and Samson's fall and misery had been inter-
nalized, with the result that the mere physical aspects of his
fall—his loss of strength, his imprisonment and enslavement
—were minimized; while the spiritual aspects of his ruin—his
inner mental anguish—and his blindness (which was thought
of as a spiritual symbol, the consequence and manifestation of
mentis caecitas) were magnified and given increased emphasis.
Thus Richard Rogers spoke of "*Samson* sitting in the irksome
prison in paine of body, but greater of mind," and Bishop
Hall declared that, for Samson in this misery, "death is no
punishment," and therefore "his soule shall flie foorth in this
bitternesse, without pain," for "oppression is able to make a
wise man mad: and the greater the courage is, the more pain-

---

[3] *Op.cit.*, pp. 271ff.
[4] P. 466, col. 2. In the Preface to *Samson Agonistes* Milton mentions the
fact that David Pareus had treated the Book of Revelations as a tragedy.

full the insultation."[5] Further evidence of this change whereby Samson's tragedy was thought of more often in terms of spiritual suffering resulting from failure in duty to God is found in the fact that a number of these later commentaries clearly accepted the manner of his dying as being in keeping with his divine calling. In pulling down the temple upon the Philistines and himself he fulfilled at last the vocation in which he had previously failed—as Johann Brenz put it, "Moritur in fide et vocatione Dei."[6]

It must be remembered, too, that in Milton's age the association of Samson with Hercules and Christ probably buttressed the reasonableness of his being considered a fit subject for tragedy. Sophocles' *Trachiniae* and the *Christus Patiens* attributed to Gregory Nazianzen are but two notable tragic treatments of Hercules, of whom Samson was supposed to be the original, and of Christ, whom Samson was thought to have prefigured. In the fifteenth, sixteenth, and seventeenth centuries, hardly less than throughout the Middle Ages, saints' lives and the stories of martyrs were still popular, and they were all necessarily tragic in structure.

For whatever reasons, it is clear that an extensive tragic literature had grown up about Samson before the earliest date at which Milton could have begun writing *Samson Agonistes*. Besides such non-dramatic tragedies as the *De Casibus Virorum Illustrium* of Boccaccio and its many descendants, there were a number of tragic dramas written during the Renaissance in Latin and the vernacular languages with Samson as subject. Many of these plays are no longer extant, some were never printed, most of them were probably poor things which could not have influenced Milton; but, taken collectively, they prove beyond doubt that Samson was widely and frequently treated as a tragic hero before Milton.

One of the earliest of these tragedies is the fifteenth-century French *Sanxon* in *Le Mistere du Viel Testament*, but

[5] Rogers, *Commentary*, p. 769; Hall, *Contemplations*, III, 276ff.
[6] *In Librum Iudicum et Ruth*, p. 230. A similar gloss is given in "Breeches" Bible, *in loc.* Judges 16:25, 28, 30.

there was an anonymous mystery play in German about Samson at almost the same time, and a Spanish *Auto de Sanson* is thought to date from the beginning of the sixteenth century.[7] There is also a *Tragödia des Richter Simson* (1561) attributed to Hans Sachs. And there are five known Samson tragedies in Latin in this period, beginning with Hieronymus Ziegler's *Samson*, printed in *Dramata Sacra* (Basel, 1547), and including the *Samson Tragoedia Nova* of Andreas Fabricius, the *Simson Tragoedia ad Imitationem Senecae et Antiquorum* (Heidelberg, 1600),[8] the *Simson Tragoedia Sacra* (Strassburg, 1604) of Andreas Wunstius,[9] and the Samson play in Jacobus Cornelius Lummenaeus' *Musae Lacrymantes, sive Pleias Tragica* (1628). In Italian vernacular drama the earliest play based on Samson seems to have been Alessandro Roselli's *La Reppresentazione di Sansone* (Florence, 1551).[10] At the beginning of the seventeenth century Bernardo Sandrinelli's *Sansone Accecato da' Filistei* was performed in Venice by the Congregazione dell' Oratoria della Madonna della Fava, and Vincento Giattini's *Il Sansone*, a *dialogo per musica*, was printed in Palermo in 1638.[11] Near the middle

<hr/>

[7] The French *Sanxon* may be found in *Le Mistere du Viel Testament*, ed. James de Rothschild (Paris, 1882), IV, 1-48. All the bibliographical information about the plays mentioned in this paragraph is taken from the following sources: Lione Allacci, *Dramaturgia* (Venice, 1755), cols. 236, 693f.; Cayetano Alberti de la Barrera y Leirado, *Catálogo Bibliográfico del Teatro Antiguo Español* (Madrid, 1860), p. 343; Luigi Riccoboni, *Histoire du Théâtre Italien* (Paris, 1728), p. 151; Rothschild, *op.cit.*, IV, i-xiii; H. Carrington Lancaster, *A History of French Dramatic Literature in the Seventeenth Century* (Baltimore and Paris, 1929), I, 74, 81f.; Alfred Harbage, *Annals of English Drama* (Philadelphia, 1940), pp. 38f., 72f.; Johannes Bolte, ed., *Coligny, Gustaf Adolf, Wallenstein: drei zeitgenössische lateinische Dramen von Rhodius, Narssius, Vernulaeus* (Leipzig, 1933), p. xi; Karl Goedeke, *Grundriss* (Dresden, 1886), II, 144; Leicester Bradner, "A Check-list of Original Neo-Latin Dramas by Continental Writers Printed before 1650," *PMLA*, LVIII (1945), 621-33.

[8] Subsequent editions: 1602, 1607, 1614, 1615, 1619, 1625.

[9] A German translation of this play by Wolfert Spangenberg (*Simson: ein geystlich Tragödia, darinnen ein Exempel treuhertziger Lieb zwischen Rechten Eleuten fürgebildet wird*) was printed at Strassburg in the same year.

[10] Subsequent editions: 1571, 1588, 1600?, 1608, 1611, 1616, 1617, 1620, 1641, 1678.

[11] Professor Allan H. Gilbert has informed me that Luigi Groto's *La*

of the seventeenth century Samson came again into Spanish dramatic literature in the *El Valiente Nazareno Sanson* of Juan Pérez de Montalbán, printed in Madrid in 1638, and the *Sanson* of Francisco de Rojas y Zorilla, performed in Madrid in 1641, but probably never printed. There were three Dutch tragedies in the seventeenth century which dealt with Samson: Claude de Grieck's *Samson of Edelmoedigen Nazareen Treurspel*, Abraham de Coningh's *Simpsons Treurspel*, and Joost van den Vondel's well known *Samson of de Heylige Vrack Treurspel*. The only extant French tragedy about Samson in the seventeenth century is the anonymous *Tragedie Nouuelle de Samson le Fort*, printed at Rouen *circa* 1612.[12] In English drama we know of an anonymous Samson play acted at the Red Lion Inn (1567) and another Samson play, sometimes attributed to Edward Jubye and Samuel Rowley, acted at the Admiral's Theatre in 1602; but neither play is extant.[13]

Of all the surviving plays mentioned here, Milton's critics have noticed only the one by Vondel. This fact alone makes it patently ridiculous to claim this single work as a source for *Samson Agonistes* until all the extant plays have been studied. These plays would at least yield further knowledge of the Renaissance conception of Samson. Until this dramatic literature has been studied, we can conclude only from its quantity that Samson—the figure of Christ, the original of Hercules, the saint—was widely and often made the subject of tragedy before Milton first considered the subject.

It has long been apparent to readers of *Samson Agonistes* that Milton subordinated Samson's earlier exploits. One is aware from the beginning of the poem to the end that Milton wanted us to meet a mature, a tragic Samson. There is no mention in the poem of the episode of the foxes, and there is

---

Dalida, Tragedia Nova, printed first at Venice in 1572, did not deal with the Samson story, and that the Dalida of this tragedy is a later character.

[12] See synopsis in Lancaster, *op.cit.*, I, 81f.

[13] There is also a Danish *Samsons Faengsel*, written in 1599 by Hieronymus Justesen Ranch, printed in 1633.

only passing reference (lines 1016-17, 1064) to Samson's riddle. As Samson says himself, "My riddling days are past," and we can see clearly that this is true in every respect. Most critics have thought that Milton selected from the account of Samson in the Book of Judges only those features of the hero which would best ennoble him and render him a fit subject for tragedy. Milton probably did not make any such conscious selection. His emphasis on the later and more sober aspects of Samson's career is entirely in keeping with the whole body of the Samson tradition. Milton went the way the tradition had been going for centuries. Ever since the early part of the patristic period—primarily because of the changes of emphasis needed in his story to make it possible to absorb him in Christianity—attention had been concentrated increasingly on Samson's later career and on the more tragic aspects of his life.[14]

3

BUT it is time to return to *Samson Agonistes* itself and to inquire into a number of details of the relationship between Milton's treatment of the Samson story and the principal elements of the Samson tradition.

Milton's interpretation of Samson does not involve all of the fourfold senses of Scripture equally. There is in *Samson Agonistes* no trace at all of anagogical (i.e., theological or mystical) interpretation; and, although the poem is full of moral significance, there is no specific suggestion of what is known as tropological interpretation. There is, to be sure, one passage which is reminiscent of the many instances of the use of Samson as an *a fortiori* example, a device which had long been essential to moral interpretation. It is found in these lines of the Chorus:

[14] The omnipresence of tradition in the interpretation of Samson in all periods reveals the naïveté of those critics who have thought that Milton could have read Judges in a vacuum and written his play in a vacuum. Mr. Parker thinks, for example, that, save for Greek tragedy, the vacuum was perfect and that "there is no need to look elsewhere" (*Milton's Debt*, p. 4).

Since man on earth unparallel'd!
The rarer thy example stands,
By how much from the top of wondrous glory,
Strongest of mortal men,
To lowest pitch of abject fortune thou art fall'n. (165-69)

But—leaving allegorical interpretation temporarily out of account[15]—one can say that Milton's interpretation of the Samson story is ostensibly an example of rationalistic literal ism. Although there is nothing in the poem to suggest that Milton questioned for a moment the historicity of Samson, the poet did not scorn utterly the rationalism which was becoming increasingly useful as the seventeenth century grew older. Milton was surely one of the stalwart defenders of the literal truth of Scripture in his age, and he probably agreed with Manoa, who tried to encourage his son by reminding him that

> God who caus'd a fountain at thy prayer
> From the dry ground to spring, thy thirst to allay
> After the brunt of battel, can as easie
> Cause light again within thy eies to spring. (581-84)

There are, nevertheless, hints of rationalism in the poem. One of the things about the Samson story which drew rationalistic interpretation to the aid of literalism was the doubtfulness of Samson's being able to go in and out of Gaza and Sorek without being set upon by foes in those Philistine strongholds. Manoa, in Milton's poem, suggests that such freedom was possible because of the formidableness of Samson's divine strength. Thus he,

> with a strength
> Equivalent to Angels walk'd thir streets,
> None offering fight. (342-44)

In the description of the temple of Dagon given by the Hebrew Messenger when reporting the catastrophe, one finds a more clearly rationalistic element:

> The building was a spacious Theatre
> Half round on two main Pillars vaulted high,

[15] See below, section 5.

With seats where all the Lords and each degree
Of sort, might sit in order to behold,
The other side was op'n, where the throng
On banks and scaffolds under Skie might stand. (1605-10)

It was there on the open side, the Messenger explains, that
he was standing when Samson pulled down the

two massie Pillars
That to the arched roof gave main support. (1633-34)

This unlovely expository passage was introduced to account
for the survival of an eye-witness who can tell the tale of the
catastrophe. It reflects also a tendency to explain the marvel-
lous which is characteristic of rationalistic exegesis. If one com-
pares the floor-plan of the temple of Dagon provided in Arias
Montanus' *De Varia Republica* (Plate III) with this Miltonic
description of the same building, it can be seen that both are
attempts to show how it was possible for Samson to destroy
the entire structure by overturning "two main Pillars." Both
explanations spring alike from a desire to preserve the validity
of the literal sense of Scripture.

Like all who interpreted the story throughout seventeen
centuries, Milton treated Samson as a hero. Manoa and the
Chorus of Danites recall with poignant regret the late indignities suffered by

That Heroic, that Renown'd,
Irresistible *Samson*, whom unarm'd
No strength of man, or fiercest wild beast could withstand;
Who tore the Lion, as the Lion tears the Kid,
Ran on embattelld Armies clad in Iron,
And weaponless himself,
Made Arms ridiculous. (125-31)

And Samson is depicted as a hero of high and serious purpose.
Milton sided with the many commentators who had declared
that Samson's exploits against the Philistines were warfare,
not just the pranks of an adventurous bully; for Milton has
Manoa refer to Samson as a "single combatant" against the
Philistines, who

> Duell'd thir Armies rank't in proud array,
> Himself an Army. (345-46)

And the Chorus says that only those who "stood aloof" were safe

> When insupportably his foot advanc't,
> In scorn of thir proud arms and warlike tools,
> Spurn'd them to death by Troops. (136-38)

Samson's earlier feats are either omitted (e.g., the episode of the foxes) or recounted in such glowingly martial terms as those used in the lines just quoted, and every resource of the story is bent to present Samson in the character of the promised deliverer of Israel. Many commentators had remarked that in foretelling the birth of Samson the angel of God had said only that the son would "begin to deliver" Israel from bondage. Milton allows Samson a more positive statement of his own mission:

> Promise was that I
> Should *Israel* from *Philistian* yoke deliver, (38-39)

says Samson at the opening of the tragedy; and the Chorus takes up the same theme near the end of the poem:

> Living or dying thou hast fulfill'd
> The work for which thou wast foretold
> To *Israel.* (1661-63)

This work, of course, was fulfilled only by Samson's final deed. For a time he seemed to have failed utterly in his mission. But even in his earlier life, as Milton depicts him, Samson had been wholly devoted to his great vocation. Milton lets Samson give good reasons for all his acts. Samson tells us, for example, that when he retired to the Rock of Etham he was

> Not flying, but fore-casting in what place
> To set upon them, what advantag'd best. (254-55)

Moreover, Milton heightens the irony of Samson's situation by allowing him to complain justly of the treacherous repudiation he had suffered at the hands of

> *Israel's* Governours, and Heads of Tribes,
> Who seeing those great acts which God had done
> Singly by me against their Conquerours
> Acknowledg'd not, or not at all consider'd
> Deliverance offerd. (242-46)

And many critics have thought that this theme is evidence
that Milton meant the poem in whole or in part as a political
preachment addressed to the English nation after the Restoration. One cannot deny that such lines were acutely pertinent
to the England of 1671, especially from the point of view of
John Milton, who had spent many years of his life and
squandered his sight in the cause of winning liberty for those
who knew not how to preserve it.

> But what more oft in Nations grown corrupt,
> And by thir vices brought to servitude,
> Then to love Bondage more then Liberty,
> Bondage with ease then strenuous liberty? (268-71)

This hits close to home. But the critics who have stressed this
feature of *Samson Agonistes* have usually assumed that this
was something new which Milton himself injected into the
story. Nothing could be further from the truth. There is not
precisely the same element in the Book of Judges, it is true.
Yet even there one finds a constant reiteration of the Deuteronomic conception of the book's significance. It was a time,
we are told, when the Israelites "went a-whoring after other
Gods," and "forsook the Lord God of their fathers," and
"served Baal and Ashtaroth," and "did evil in the sight of
the Lord." In the Deuteronomic redaction, the stories of
Judges were all made to show that it was by their vices that
the Israelites were brought to servitude, and in numerous
commentaries in the Middle Ages and the Renaissance the
Christian writers repeatedly emphasized the religious, moral,
and political indigence of the Jews in Samson's time. One of
the principal features of the literal interpretation of Scripture
as it descended from the earliest Fathers was its interest in
the historicity of all that was recorded in the Bible. The annalists and chroniclers all accepted Samson as an historical

figure and paid most attention to the political significance of
his career. Milton did not invent the political overtones of
Samson's story, nor did he make changes in the material to
make those overtones clearer. They were an integral part of
the Samson tradition.[16] The most that we can say confidently
of the political import of *Samson Agonistes* is that Milton
found the tradition formed in such a way as to highlight—
among many other elements—the political interest inherent
in Samson's story; and, with a nice appreciation of contemporary applicability, he kept that element intact in his poem.
But any attempt on the part of critics to make political allegory the heart of this poem is indefensible.

Accepting Samson as a hero appointed by God to be the
liberator of Israel, Milton also represented Samson's strength
as supernatural, a gift from God to be employed in His service. At several points in the poem it is said that Samson was
strengthened and impelled by God, and Samson himself spoke
of his "Heav'n-gifted strength" (line 36). This, too, comes
from the extra-biblical tradition rather than from the account
of Samson in the Book of Judges. There we are told only
that "the Spirit of the Lord began to move him at times in
the camp of Dan" (13:25); that his desire to marry the
woman of Timnath "was of the Lord" (14:4); that "the

---

[16] By the vast majority of Christian writers in all periods Samson was
regarded primarily as a ruler and deliverer of Israel. The historio-political
emphasis was nearly always inseparable from literal interpretation. See, for
example, Clement of Alexandria, *Stromata*, I, xxi (*Pat. Graec.*, VIII, 838);
Sulpicius Severus, *Chronica*, I, 27 (*Corp. Script. Eccles. Lat.*, I, 30f.); Isi-
dore of Seville, *Pat. Lat.*, LXXXII, 278f., LXXXIII, 389, and LXXXIII, 139;
Chronicon Paschale (*Pat. Graec.*, XCII, 238); Cyril of Alexandria, *Contra
Julianum*, I (*Pat. Graec.*, LXXVI, 519); Bede, *Quaestiones super Librum
Judicum*, viii (*Pat. Lat.*, XCIII, 428ff.); Georgius Hamartolus, *Chronicon*
(*Pat. Graec.*, CX, 202ff.); Georgius Cedrenus, *Compendium Historiarum*
(*Pat. Graec.*, CXXI, 135-38); Ælfric, *EETS*, original series, no. 160, p.
33f.; Petrus Comestor, *Historia*, xvi-xix (*Pat. Lat.*, CXCVIII, 1285-90);
Joannes Zonaras, *Annales*, I, xxiv (*Pat. Graec.*, CXXXIV, 118f.); Wyclif,
"Prolog for alle the bokis of the Bible," in *The Holy Bible in the Earliest
English Version*, ed. Forshall and Madden (Oxford, 1850); Michaelis
Glyca, *Annales*, II (*Pat. Graec.*, CLVIII, 315-22); Peter Martyr, *In Librum
Iudicum*, pp. 135-59; Arias Montanus, *De Varia Republica*, pp. 499-580;
Salianus, *Annales*, II, 441-72; Torniellus, *Annales*, I, 411-14; and Hugo
Grotius, *Annotationes in Vetus Testamentum*, p. 203f.

Spirit of the Lord came mightily upon him" when he tore
apart the lion (14:6); that again when the "Spirit of the
Lord came upon him" he slew thirty men in Askalon (14:19);
that yet again, so impelled, he broke the bonds with which the
Jews had bound him (15:14); and finally that Samson called
upon God to strengthen him in the temple of Dagon (16:28).
But the biblical wording is not very specific, not nearly so
specific as it was made in the commentaries, where it was put
into technical, doctrinal terms by such important writers as
Ambrose, Augustine, Cyril of Alexandria, Peter Lombard,
Thomas Aquinas, Thomas Hayne, and Cornelius à Lapide,
among a number of others.[17] In this, as in many other respects,
Samson Agonistes has about it a rich aura of ancient connotations which are invisible to readers who are unaware of the
tradition behind it, the tradition which was very real to Milton and to the audience he sought.[18]

[17] Ambrose, *De Spiritu Sancto* (*Pat. Lat.*, XVI, 774ff.); Augustine, *Sermo
CCCLXIV*, paragraph 1 (*Pat. Lat.*, XXXIX, 1639); Cyril of Alexandria, *De
Sancta et Consubstantiali Trinitate* (*Pat. Graec.*, LXXV, 1094), and *In
Librum Judicum Homiliae* (*Pat. Graec.*, LXXV, 1131); Peter Lombard,
Collectanea in Epistolas Sancti Pauli (*Pat. Lat.*, CXCII, 497); Thomas
Aquinas, *Summa Theologiae*, II, ii, ques. 174, art. 3; Thomas Hayne, *General View of the Holy Scriptures*, p. 217f.; Cornelius à Lapide, *Commentarius in Ioshue, Iudicum, Ruth*, p. 175.
[18] Milton did not clearly take sides in the old dispute as to the exact
location of Samson's strength. The earliest commentators had believed that
his strength really resided in his hair, but most of the later commentators
were of the opinion that Samson's unshorn hair was merely symbolic of
his faith and of his adherence to his Nazaritic vows. At one place in Milton's poem Samson says,

> God, when he gave me strength, to shew withal,
> How slight the gift was, hung it in my Hair. (58-59)

But later, when Harapha taunts Samson with the notion that his strength
lay in his hair, Samson replies,

> My trust is in the living God who gave me
> At my Nativity this strength, diffus'd
> No less through all my sinews, joints and bones,
> Then thine, while I preserv'd these locks unshorn,
> The pledge of my unviolated vow. (1140-44)

These two statements appear to be contradictory, and they reflect two opposed views in biblical exegesis. Samson's first statement in the opening,
expository section of the poem probably expresses what was still the popular
understanding in the seventeenth century (as now) of the nature of Samson's strength. Those completely unlearned in the literature of exegesis

Milton not only depicted his hero as one sent to deliver Israel from bondage and strengthened for that purpose by the indwelling of the Holy Spirit; he also accepted explicitly the time-honored conception of Samson as God's agent and champion,

> from some great act
> Or benefit reveal'd to *Abraham's* race. (28-29)

Samson himself gives the same argument for this interpretation as had been urged by all the commentators:

> O wherefore was my birth from Heaven foretold
> Twice by an Angel, (23-24)

if not to herald God's designated instrument? He was, he asserts, God's

> nursling once and choice delight,
> His destin'd from the womb.[19]

According to Samson's own statements in the poem, all his deeds were performed in that capacity. Indeed, Milton had Samson give the interpretation of himself which had by that time become standard among the exegetes: it was not Samson who acted, but God who acted through him—

> those great acts which God had done
> Singly by me against their Conquerours. (243-44)

Samson is particularly positive about this contention when he answers Harapha's imputation that he was just "a Murtherer, a Revolter, and a Robber":

---

would have expected such a statement as Samson makes at first. But by the time they had followed Milton's Samson up to the arrival of Harapha they would be better prepared for a nicer interpretation, and one which seems more likely to represent Milton's own opinion. However, if this is really an inconsistency at all, it is one of no importance; Milton was writing a tragedy, not an exegetical tract.

[19] Lines 633-34. The phrase "from the womb" was heavily laden with rich connotations for a reader acquainted with the Vulgate or the Latin Bible of Junius and Tremellius and with any part of hermeneutic literature, throughout which the phrase "ex utero matris" recurs like a Wagnerian *Leitmotif*, used, as it was, as evidence that Samson was a special sort of Nazarite—one designated by God in the very womb of his mother, not an ordinary, voluntary, temporary Nazarite. See also *S.A.*, lines 30-32.

> I was no private but a person rais'd
> With strength sufficient and command from Heav'n
> To free my Countrey. (1211-13)

And in this same connection Samson's tragedy is given cosmic significance:

> all the contest is now
> 'Twixt God and *Dagon*; *Dagon* hath presum'd,
> Me overthrown, to enter lists with God. (461-63)

And in the beautiful final Chorus we are told that God has returned to Samson

> And to his faithful Champion hath in place
> Bore witness gloriously. (1751-52)

In *Samson Agonistes*, as in the hermeneutic literature, many of Samson's deeds are justified on this ground. Theodoret, ages before, had argued that all of Samson's apparent waywardnesses—and he gave as an example his taking to wife the woman of Timnath—were *a Domino*;[20] and Peter Lombard and Alanus ab Insulis had urged, too, that Samson acted always at the instigation of God—even, as Thomas Aquinas agreed, in bringing about his own death.[21] In Milton's own age, Calvin, Brenz, Bullinger, Pareus, and others had defended Samson on the ground that, as Calvin put it, he "followed the guidance of God" and, "animated by His promise, undertook what was commanded."[22] In Milton's poem Samson says of his choice of the Philistine woman of Timnath for his bride:

> What I motion'd was of God; I knew
> From intimate impulse, and therefore urg'd
> The Marriage on. (222-24)

At another point in the tragedy the Chorus asserts that it was God Himself who dispensed with His own laws and

---

[20] *Quaestiones in Judices*, xxi (*Pat. Graec.*, LXXX, 510).

[21] *Collectanea in Epistolas Sancti Pauli* (*Pat. Lat.*, CXCII, 497); *De Fide Catholica contra Haereticos* (*Pat. Lat.*, CCX, 343f.); *Summa Theologiae*, II, ii, ques. 64, art. 5, paragraph 4.

[22] See above, p. 74, n. 19.

> prompted this Heroic *Nazarite*,
> Against his vow of strictest purity,
> To seek in marriage that fallacious Bride,
> Unclean, unchaste, (318-21)

that is, Dalila of Sorek. Here again, the root of a traditional interpretation lay in Judges (14:4), where Samson's desire to marry the woman of Timnath is said to be "of God." But the fit reader of Milton's day would have heard echoes in these words which, although we today are deaf to them, reminded him of the almost endless corridors of doctrine winding back through the centuries. Nearly every commentator who dealt with Samson asked why he had persisted in choosing Philistine women. In *Samson Agonistes* the Chorus raises the same question:

> I oft have heard men wonder
> Why thou shouldst wed *Philistian* women rather
> Then of thine own Tribe; (215-17)

and the answers already quoted were the same answers as had been given by the men who had often wondered.

The principal reason why they had wondered about such questions was that they were confronted with an Old Testament figure whom the Apostle Paul had named among the *electi* who came to be regarded as saints. And perhaps the principal reason why they found justification for all of Samson's deeds was the fact that they had accepted his sainthood as incontrovertible. Milton's treatment of these questions suggests a familiarity with the commentaries in which Samson was defended as he defends himself in *Samson Agonistes*; and Milton could not have perused such arguments without being aware that they were used to buttress Samson's sainthood. If, as has been claimed, Milton had intended to depart from the well-established conception of Samson as saint, he would have had to write some disclaimer into the poem. Since one finds no such disclaimer in the poem and since one does find the orthodox arguments for Samson's sainthood in the poem, one must conclude that Milton did not abandon the view of Samson as saint in using him as the hero of tragedy.

In this connection one should pause to examine another passage in *Samson Agonistes* which is enriched by familiarity with the Christian tradition. In lines 277-85 the Chorus responds to Samson's complaint against the lassitude of his people by saying:

> Thy words to my remembrance bring
> How *Succoth* and the Fort of *Penuel*
> Thir great Deliverer contemn'd,
> The matchless *Gideon* in pursuit
> Of *Madian* and her vanquisht Kings:
> And how ingrateful *Ephraim*
> Had dealt with *Jephtha*, who by argument,
> Not worse then by his shield and spear
> Defended *Israel* from the *Ammonite*.

This comparison of Samson with Gideon and Jephtha is nearly lost upon the reader of today, even if he knows the stories of the other two heroes. To a seventeenth-century reader, however, the comparison must have seemed especially appropriate because all three were saints as well as military heroes: Gideon and Jephtha had also been mentioned by Paul in the Epistle to the Hebrews, and countless times thereafter in the literature of Christianity these names had been linked in this way, always with the Epistle to the Hebrews as part of the connotation. Here again one must conclude that Milton would not have risked such connotations had he wished to depart from the conception of Samson as saint which they perpetuated.[23]

---

[23] In lines 1287-96, the Chorus names patience as the trait which usually distinguishes saints and prophesies that Samson will ultimately be honored for that virtue; and then in line 1623, the Hebrew Messenger, relating the catastrophe, reports that Samson was "patient but undaunted." See also lines 1310-42, 1408-9, and 1624-28. This discussion of the sort of performance which Samson was to give in the temple reflects a problem which had long troubled the commentators. Accepting Samson as a saint, they wondered what sort of feats he could have performed at the festival of Dagon without acting in a manner indecorous in a saint, a Nazarite, a champion of God. Some of the commentators suggested that perhaps Samson pulled down the columns before the time came for his part in the program, thus saving him from an undignified display of his strength before God's enemies. It is interesting to notice that Milton did not adopt this explanation. Did he eschew it in the interest of more intense pathos and irony, the exemplification of the lowest depths of Samson's fall before he rose to

But to Milton—as to all the commentators who accepted Samson as a saint—it was plain that Samson had fallen temporarily from saintly ways, had sinned and forfeited his divine strength as a result of that sin. Repeatedly in the poem we are told that Samson was himself to blame for his fall.

> What if all foretold
> Had been fulfilld but through mine own default,
> Whom have I to complain of but my self? (44-46)

says he in his opening speech; and later, after the Chorus has recalled his previous exploits, he blames himself again,

> Who like a foolish Pilot have shipwrack't,
> My Vessel trusted to me from above. (198-99)

At another time he speaks of himself in terms which suggest the tragic fault of *hybris*, saying that he was "swoll'n with pride" when he fell because he was "fearless of danger" and, "like a petty God,"

> walk'd about admir'd of all and dreaded
> On hostile ground, none daring my affront. (530-31)

This reason for Samson's fall had been given first by Josephus and had been repeated by many later writers. It is obviously one of the traditional elements in Milton's portrayal of Samson. But elsewhere in the poem Milton stresses another reason for Samson's fall which is less obviously derived from tradition. According to Manoa (lines 348-49), Samson's fault lay in his relying on his strength alone and in forgetting that it was a supernatural endowment, not his but God's; and

---

glorious triumph? It does not reduce Samson's stature as a tragic hero, nor as a religious hero: Christ, too, had borne the Cross through the streets of Jerusalem. The space given to the question in *Samson Agonistes* indicates at least that Milton was acquainted with the discussions of the problem in the commentaries.

In having Manoa sue with the Philistines for the release of his son, Milton made an innovation in the story for which there seems to have been no warrant either in Scripture or in the catena. This is, to be sure, primarily an artistic addition: it contributes to the plot by making Manoa an agent of offered choice. It also intensifies the tragic irony produced by the peripetia. Moreover it amplifies Samson's zealous heroism, his confidence in his calling as a champion of God, and his readiness as a saint to endure dark captivity with patience and suffer martyrdom with fortitude.

Manoa laments this error, exclaiming against the "ever failing trust In mortal strength." Samson, too, admits,

> Strength is my bane,
> And proves the sourse of all my miseries. (63-64)

This idea is made even more explicit by the hero when he
says,

> Immeasurable strength they might behold
> In me, of wisdom nothing more then mean;
> This with the other should, at least, have paird,
> These two proportiond ill drove me transverse. (206-9)

Such repeated statements seem to emphasize Milton's conception of Samson as the type of one strong in body but weak
in mind—an idea set forth clearly in Samson's opening speech:

> O impotence of mind, in body strong!
> But what is strength without a double share
> Of wisdom, vast, unwieldy, burdensom,
> Proudly secure, yet liable to fall
> By weakest suttleties, not made to rule,
> But to subserve where wisdom bears command. (52-57)

It was this "impotence of mind" which caused Samson's
"shameful garrulity," led him to give up his "fort of silence"
to Dalila; Dalila herself "was not the prime cause, but I my
self" (234). This aspect of Samson has often been magnified
by the critics, who have regarded the emphasis on mentality
as a peculiarly Miltonic innovation in the Samson story. And,
on the surface, that element in *Samson Agonistes* does appear
to be a Miltonic invention. However it is entirely in keeping
with the whole of the Samson tradition, for the commentators
had always written of Samson as having been notable primarily for his great strength; strength was always the keynote of
their repetitions of his story. I have found no document in the
exegetical literature in which Samson is treated as having been
endowed with remarkable intellectual capacity. Milton's handling of Samson in this respect is wholly true to the tradition,
reflecting, as it does, one of the implicit assumptions of that
tradition. Of course, in the process of making a tragedy out
of Samson's story, Milton engaged in what might be termed

poetic amplification, as a result of which this element is enlarged—the stripe always looks broader and more prominent in the finished jacket than it did when seen on the bolt. In the course of bringing Samson to life in the proportions of a tragic hero, Milton made more of some features of the tradition than they might seem to have counted for in the tradition itself. Even when Milton seems to the casual reader to have invented something which is not prominent in the tradition, it is usually found that the invention is not radically new, but rather something implicit in the tradition which becomes explicit when Milton sets forth Samson as a living person.

Furthermore, Milton's insistence that it was this weakness in Samson rather than the machinations of Dalila which brought about his fall—this insistence is very close to the typical treatment of Samson's story in medieval and early Renaissance poetry. Milton has made it more specific: it was not simply because Samson consorted with women, as medieval writers had seen it, that he fell; it was because Samson revealed God's secret to a woman, told her that he was a Nazarite consecrated to God and endowed with divine strength to serve God's cause.[24]

Although Milton made it clear that Samson himself was to blame for his fall, Dalila is given a great deal of attention in *Samson Agonistes*. She is represented as deceitful, a "specious monster," and we are given to understand that she is the occasion, if not the cause, of Samson's ruin. Milton sided with the commentators who believed that Dalila was Samson's wife (lines 227, 320), but he disagreed with those who had

---

[24] Lines 201-2: "Divulg'd the secret gift of God/To a deceitful Woman." There is an interesting parallel here between Samson and the Christ of *Paradise Regained*. As Professor Pope has shown in her study of the tradition of the Temptation, one of Satan's chief purposes in tempting Christ was to find out whether Christ was the Son of God, to determine what sort of opponent he had to confront. Therefore part of the interest of *Paradise Regained* for the seventeenth-century reader was in Christ's preventing Satan from learning what he wanted to know; Christ had to parry Satan's thrusts without revealing His identity, had to conceal the very source of His power. The parallel with Samson lies in Samson's revealing his Nazariteship. Cf. Pope, *"Paradise Regained": the Tradition and the Poem* (Baltimore, 1947), pp. 31ff.

followed Cajetan in suggesting that she might have been a
Jewess. On the other hand, Milton made use of what looks
like Cajetan's interpretation when he composed Dalila's
speeches of self-justification. Cajetan had thought that perhaps the Philistines broke faith with Dalila, that she did not
bargain for as much cruelty to Samson as the satraps ultimately afflicted him with.[25] In *Samson Agonistes* (lines 790-
814) Milton allows Dalila to defend herself on the same
ground: she betrayed Samson to the satraps only because she
loved him and wanted to keep him by her constantly,

> day and night
> Mine and Loves prisoner, not the *Philistines*,
> Whole to my self, unhazarded abroad,
> Fearless at home of partners in my love.

When Samson refuses to listen to this argument, Dalila pleads
that she had long been beset by the Philistines, girt round with
sieges

> Which might have aw'd the best resolv'd of men,
> The constantest to have yielded without blame. (847-48)

But Samson is not to be deceived again; he sends her from
him in righteous anger. Like Samson, the seventeenth-century
reader would readily have perceived the speciousness of Dalila's defense of herself. For she had a bad name in the tradition which was still alive and intact; she was well known
from poem, broadside, and sermon as a deceitful, a treacherous, a dangerously clever sort of woman, skillful in blandish-
ment and importunity. The readers for whom Milton wrote
probably reacted to Dalila as they reacted to Satan or Belial:
they were prepared for a Devil equipped with what appear on
the surface to be the best of arguments. And it must have
seemed especially fitting to Protestant Englishmen in the
seventeenth century to find the Devil in the person of Dalila
citing a prominent Popish commentator for his purpose.

The strong element of anti-feminism which revolves about
Dalila in *Samson Agonistes* has usually been considered a spe-

[25] *Opera* (London, 1637), II, 63.

cially Miltonic twist and has often been adduced—along with
the strictures on politics and the poignant passages dealing
with blindness—as evidence that the poem is to be understood
primarily as an autobiographical document.[26] There is, un-
doubtedly, a powerful anti-feminist strain in the poem, some
of which (e.g., lines 1046-49) seem intensely personal to a
modern reader; and it may be true that the emphasis on this
feature of the Samson story resulted entirely from Milton's
personal experience with Mary Powell in early life. But it
need not have. This element had always been persistent in
the Samson tradition, had been stressed by many writers from
the time of Ambrose's letter to Bishop Vigilius. It was particularly characteristic of late medieval poetic treatments of the
Samson story, in which, as has already been shown, Samson's
love for Dalila and her betrayal of him were at the very center of the story's interest. This medieval conception of the
fall of Samson is even more purely set forth by Shakespeare,
Spenser, Gascoigne, Burton, Phineas Fletcher, and Quarles.
Do we argue from such evidence that all these writers were
misogynists? Or, if not, do we measure the autobiographical
content of Milton's poetry by a unique standard? Considering, too, the happiness of Milton's later marital experience,
one finds it far more reasonable to suppose that the anti-feminism in _Samson Agonistes_ was traditional rather than personal.[27]

Even though Dalila is shown to be a "specious monster," it
is clear that Milton represented Samson as having fallen

[26] See lines 50-51, 202, 236, 379, 1010-49, 1053-60.
[27] In the popular ballads and broadsides of the early modern period, too,
the Samson story took the form of the fall of a great man caused by an
evil woman. See _The Shirburn Ballads_, ed. A. Clark (Oxford, 1907), pp.
41-47; "A Most Excellent and Famous Ditty of Sampson, Judge of Israel"
(1586), in _Roxburghe Ballads_ (Hartford, 1874), II, 459-64; _The Pepys
Ballads_, ed. H. E. Rollins (Cambridge, Mass., 1929), I, 43, and VI, 311.
See also the ragged doggerel on Samson in Simon Wastell, _Microbiblion,
or the Bibles Epitome_ (London, 1629), p. 52f. Judging from the evidence
of the ballads and broadsides, which Milton, too, might well have had some
acquaintance with, Samson was, indeed, "sung and proverb'd for a Fool/
In every street," as he himself says in lines 203-4. These lines may allude
to those ballads and broadsides.

through his own fault. And it is clear, as well, that Milton, like the commentators who raised and discussed the question, depicted Samson as one who repented during his captivity. Repentance is expressed in nearly every utterance of Samson in the poem. He has been humbled, and he is now thoroughly ashamed of his former pride, his reliance on mere physical prowess, his garrulity and weakness in revealing God's secret. Manoa even counsels him not to carry his penitence to the point of self-punishment (lines 502-15). But while Samson is deeply aware of his own guilt, he does have the penitent believer's confidence in God's readiness to restore him to grace; he is penitent, but he has not lost faith.

> These evils I deserve and more,
> Acknowledge them from God inflicted on me
> Justly, yet despair not of his final pardon
> Whose ear is ever open; and his eye
> Gracious to re-admit the suppliant. (1169-73)

This whole conception of a repentant Samson was an extra-biblical Christian theory distributed widely throughout hermeneutic literature. It does not come from the Book of Judges; it would be going out of one's way to argue that it comes from Greek tragedy.[28]

The Samson whom we meet in Milton's play is a saint, a champion of God, a great hero, who, through his own fault, has failed in his high vocation, fallen from virtue and grace, and sorely repented.

Although we meet in *Samson Agonistes* a fallen hero, the poet devotes a good deal of space to reminding us from how great a height that hero has fallen. Samson himself tells us in the moving speech which opens the poem (lines 1-114); the Chorus of his tribesmen can hardly believe the change that has come over their noble and glorious hero (lines 115-75); Manoa, too, is deeply struck with the "miserable change"

---

[28] Manoa gives the same reason for believing that God had recognized Samson's repentance and restored him to grace as had been given by all the commentators: Samson's consecrated hair and his divine strength were restored (lines 1495-1503).

which has befallen his son (lines 340-72); and even Harapha's words emphasize the painful contrast between what
Samson once was and what he is now (lines 1082-90, 1092-
1103). In fact, Milton allows Manoa (lines 368-72, 430-31)
and the Chorus (lines 687-91) to remark—as Salianus had
done[29]—that the misery which Samson has suffered is out of
proportion to his fault, "too grievous for the trespass." This
was an element of the tradition especially appropriate for
Milton to adopt because it intensifies tragic *catharsis*, as he
must have been aware.[30] This misery of the fallen Samson,
revealed in his every utterance, consists mostly of mental and
spiritual anguish. He speaks of suffering "the tumors of a
troubl'd mind" (line 185), and of "the anguish of my Soul"
(line 458); and Manoa tries to comfort him by suggesting
that his premonitions of death arise from "anguish of the
mind" (line 600). By 1671 the reading public would have
expected to find this emphasis in a serious poem about Samson. As early as 1592 Samson's reputation as one characterized
by dejection and painful mental anguish was well enough established to allow Thomas Nashe to use *sampsown* as a verb
meaning "cast down in dejection and anguished thought."[31]
And attention has already been called to the writings of Richard Rogers and Joseph Hall, in which Samson's pain of mind
was stressed.[32] It was this mental suffering more than any
merely physical pain which made Samson long for death.
Rogers had said of him: "Death is no punishment," for "his
soule shall flie foorth in this bitternesse, without pain." And
Milton's Samson cries out,

[29] *Annales* (Cologne, 1620), II, 466, col. 2.

[30] The familiar remark of Aristotle (*Poetics*, 13) that pity is aroused by
a misfortune that is undeserved or out of proportion to the hero's fault, was,
of course, the *locus classicus* of this conception; and Aristotle was, perhaps,
the source of the conception for both Milton and Salianus.

[31] *Works*, ed. R. B. McKerrow (London, 1904), I, 256: "And I wonder
verie much, that you *sampsownd* not your selfe into a consumption with the
profound cogitation of it." McKerrow did not connect the word with
Judges, but the etymology here suggested seems a reasonable one. So far
as I know, Nashe used it as a nonce-word.

[32] See above, p. 77.

> Hopeless are all my evils, all remediless;
> This one prayer yet remains, might I be heard,
> No long petition, speedy death,
> The close of all my miseries, and the balm. (648-51)

And again:

> But come what will, my deadliest foe will prove
> My speediest friend, by death to rid me hence,
> The worst that he can give, to me the best. (1262-64)

Of course, Samson's mental suffering is aggravated by his physical helplessness, and especially by his blindness. Nor can it be denied that Milton communicated the intense pathos of blindness more vividly than any writer possessed of sight could have done. Numerous writers before Milton had discussed Samson's blindness, had described its torments, had interpreted it tropologically as the outward manifestation of the blindness of mind defined by Gregory the Great, and had even called attention to the tragic fitness of Samson's being afflicted in the part which had offended by leading him to break his Nazaritic vows. But the particular tone and terror of what Milton gives Samson to say about the darkness which encompasses him even in "the blaze of noon" is undeniably Milton's own.[33]

Milton depicted the fallen Samson as one whose anguish could be relieved only by death, but he did not portray him

---

[33] One learns from a study of the Samson tradition that Milton's monumental line, "Eyeless in *Gaza* at the Mill with slaves," is full of ancient echoes and that for this reason it was probably an even richer line for Milton and his contemporaries than it is for us. Throughout the hermeneutic literature there are phrases which this line calls to the mind of the reader who is steeped in that literature: "Postquam oculos perdidit, ad molam deputatus est" (Gregory, *Pat. Lat.*, LXXIX, 790); "quod captivatus, quod caecatus, quod ad molam deputatus est" (Bede, *Pat. Lat.*, XCIII, 430); see also Cyprian, *Corp. Script. Eccles. Lat.*, XXIII, 206; *Chronicon Paschale*, *Pat. Graec.*, XCII, 238; Petrus Comestor, *Historia Scholastica, Pat. Lat.*, CXCVIII, 1290; Strabo, *Glossa Ordinaria, Pat. Lat.*, CXIII, 532; Hugo of St. Victor, *Adnotatiunculae, Pat. Lat.*, CLXXV, 263; Abelard, *Planctus Israel super Samson*, lines 17-19, *Pat. Lat.*, CLXXVIII, 1820; Schmidt on Judges 16:21, *In Librum Judicum*, p. 1297; Torniellus, *Annales*, p. 412, col. 1; Rupert of St. Heribert, *In Librum Judicum*, xxiv, *Pat. Lat.*, CLXVII, 1054; Marbecke, *Lyues of the Holy Sainctes*, p. 72; Rogers, *Commentary*, p. 765; Patrick, *Commentary*, p. 561.

as a suicide. In this, Milton was in accord with nearly all the commentators who had striven to defend Samson the saint against the charge implied by his final prayer, "Moriatur anima mea cum Philistinis," and by his pulling down the temple to destroy the Philistines and himself. Milton clearly took sides with the overwhelming majority of the commentators who regarded Samson's last prayer as an utterance of self-sacrifice in the cause of God and Samson's death under the roof of the temple as a martyrdom. Milton avoided a verbatim report of the prayer by having the Messenger say only that Samson

> stood, as one who pray'd,
> Or some great matter in his mind revolv'd. (1637-38)

At the end of the "Argument" prefixed to *Samson Agonistes*, Milton spoke of "what *Samson* had done to the *Philistines*, and by accident to himself"; and this interpretation is repeated by the Messenger, who tells how

> *Samson* with these immixt, inevitably
> Pulld down the same destruction on himself. (1657-58)

The Chorus reiterates the explanation immediately afterwards, saying that now, among Jehovah's enemies slain by him, the hero lies,

> self-kill'd
> Not willingly, but tangl'd in the fold
> Of dire necessity, whose law in death conjoin'd
> Thee with thy slaughter'd foes.[34]

[34] Lines 1664-67. In Milton's setting of the catastrophe there is a minor reflection of the Christian tradition. There had long been a quarrel among the commentators as to whether the festival of the Philistines at the time of Samson's death was a regular religious observance or whether it was a special feast of thanksgiving to celebrate the capture of Samson. It was not a question of doctrinal importance, but it had often been discussed. Milton chose to regard the celebration as a "Feast . . . proclaim'd by the *Philistins* as a day of Thanksgiving for thir deliverance from the hands of Samson" ("Argument," and cf. lines 433-47). This choice of the one of two traditional interpretations followed the classical principle of economy and also permitted Milton to wring more tragic irony from the predicament of Samson: it is deeply humiliating for the hero to take part in the celebration of his own ruin; and it also greatly enhances Samson's final triumph by allowing him to destroy the Philistines on the very occasion of the merrymaking at his expense. The peripetia is doubled thereby. It is satisfying to

The space given in Milton's poem to the emphasis of this interpretation of Samson's death would seem to indicate that he was aware of the importance given to this question of suicide in the exegetical literature about Samson, and the insistence with which it is urged makes it even more difficult to see in Milton's poem any departure from the established conception of Samson as saint.[35]

4

CRITICS have paid little attention to the epithet *Agonistes* which Milton applied to Samson in the title of the tragedy. Bishop Newton thought that the term was used to designate Samson as an actor, or as one represented in a play. Dunster eschewed Newton's interpretation and declared that *Agonistes* refers to Samson's being brought forth "to exhibit his athletick powers." Dunster also remarked that the epithet served to define the scope of the play, just as Aeschylus distinguished *Prometheus Bound* from *Prometheus Unbound.*[36] Masson accepted Dunster's interpretation and simply noted in passing that *Agonistes* means "the Agonist, Athlete or Wrestler."[37] Verity repeated this gloss, adding that *Agonistes* means "a combatant at public games" and that it emphasizes "the main aspect under which Samson appears," namely, "as wrestler

---

come so close to observing a great poet in the very act of artistic choice, of selecting the one traditional interpretation which is artistically most effective.

[35] Some seventeenth-century readers would probably have found an allusion to exegetical writings in the last speech of Manoa, who says that he will erect a suitable monument for Samson,

> With all his Trophies hung, and Acts enroll'd
> In copious Legend, or sweet Lyric Song. (1736-37)

There was no such mention of monument or epitaph in the Book of Judges, but an epitaph for Samson was set forth in Salianus' *Annales* (1620) and reprinted in Cornelius à Lapide's *Commentarius in Ioshue, Iudicum, Ruth* (1664). See above, p. 66. The word *legend*, as used in these lines, was the name of a literary genre, of course, and designated a saint's life—another indication that Milton did not depart from the conception of Samson as saint.

[36] Todd, ed., *Works of Milton*, v, 343.

[37] *Works of Milton*, II, 582.

before the assembled Philistines."[38] Professor Hughes perpetuated this venerable interpretation in his recent edition of the tragedy. "*Agonistes*," he says, "transliterates the Greek name for the amateur athletes who competed in the public games, and it refers to Samson's appearance at the festival of the Philistines in the temple of Dagon at the climax of the tragedy, when he wrestles with the pillars there."[39] Professor Parker, however, has declared that Samson Agonistes is "more than Samson the Wrestler," reminding us that *Agonistes* means also "an advocate, an actor, and a champion." He even suggests that when Milton used the epithet he may have had in mind the English words *agony* and *agonize*. But he concludes his consideration of the title by confessing that he regards such attempts to interpret *Agonistes* as "futile guesses."[40]

There is, however, ample evidence in both Graeco-Roman and Christian traditions to enable us to find a more accurate and meaningful interpretation of the title of Milton's tragedy than these, and without resort to guesswork. In fact, when one approaches it with the Christian tradition in mind, the title is like a wide gate opening upon the total meaning of the poem. I shall try here to show that when Milton used the epithet *Agonistes* he probably intended it both to denote a specific conception of Samson and to connote a view of life which was then twenty-three centuries old. In order to regain the now-forgotten connotations of *Agonistes*, it is necessary to examine the history of a group of Greek and Latin words and to consider their significance in Christian literature and Christian doctrine during the Middle Ages and the Reformation.

Agonistes is, as Professor Hughes has said, a transliteration of the Greek word ἀγωνιστής, which was in turn derived from the word ἀγών. The earliest meanings of ἀγών were purely literal: it denoted (1) a gathering or assembly to see games, (2) the arena itself where the games were held, or (3) the contest for a prize at public games. However, like many such

---

[38] *Milton's "Samson Agonistes*," p. 60.
[39] P. 537, n. 1.
[40] *Milton's Debt to Greek Tragedy*, p. 13.

words, ἀγών and its synonyms and derivatives soon acquired, by extension, metaphorical meanings which ultimately supplanted the literal; hence ἀγών was widely used to denote (4) any struggle or trial, but increasingly (5) a spiritual struggle, an inner conflict. The word ἆθλον, too, which in its older form (ἄεθλον) had meant simply a physical combat, came to be used only in the sense of "spiritual struggle."[41]

The grounds of this semantic amelioration can be found in Greek philosophic writings. Among the fragments of the pre-Socratics, for example, there is an elegy by Xenophanes, the poet-philosopher of the sixth century, in which is stated for the first time the ideal of philosophic wisdom in explicit opposition to the ideal of mere physical prowess. Looking upon athletes performing in the games, Xenophanes was filled with contempt, and in this elegy he expressed his conviction that mere quickness of foot would never suffice to establish order and justice in the state. Using the terminology of the public games metaphorically, he pleaded for the inception of a new ideal which would exalt and reward athletes of the mind and spirit rather than athletes of the body. These philosopher-athletes, he argued—not the runners, the wrestlers, and the horsemen—should be granted the most generous prizes the state can provide.[42] Many Hellenists today believe that it was during the century after Xenophanes that this ideal came as near establishment as it was ever to come in the history of man. It is certain that during the great period of Greece no less a figure than the Platonic Socrates devoted his life to the doctrine that only lovers of ideas can be wise, that only the pursuit of wisdom makes human life meaningful or death understandable. Nor did Socrates think of philosophy in passive terms. In his valediction in the *Phaedo* (90e), as in

---

[41] See Liddell and Scott, *Greek-English Lexicon, in loc.*

[42]   ῥώμης γὰρ ἀμείνων
ἀνδρῶν ἠδ' ἵππων ἡμετέρη σοφίη.
ἀλλ' εἰκῇ μάλα τοῦτο νομίζεται, οὐδὲ δίκαιον
προκρίνειν ῥώμην τῆς ἀγαθῆς σοφίης.

In *Die Fragmente der Vorsokratiker*, ed. Hermann Diels and Walther Kranz, 5th ed. (Berlin, 1934), I, 129.

many other utterances, he expressed the business of the philosopher in terms of contest, struggle, or strife, urging his disciples to play the man and seek strenuously for soundness of mind (ἀνδριστέον καὶ προθυμητέον ὑγιῶς ἔχειν). The Platonic ethic favored the contemplative life, but it was to be lived in a state of intellectual and spiritual *agon*: only by extraordinary and long-continued exertion of mind and spirit could the lover of ideas hope to break through the phenomenal world to know the Good and the True. In the *Laws* (731a) the Athenian Stranger counselled his hearers to strive with all their might for virtue and wisdom, and Socrates himself concluded that unforgettable conversation recorded in the *Republic* by exhorting his followers to

hold fast ever to the heavenly way and follow after justice and virtue always, considering that the soul is immortal and able to endure every sort of good and every sort of evil. Thus shall we live dear to one another and to the gods, both while remaining here and when, like conquerors in the games [τὰ ἆθλα . . . οἱ νικηφόροι] who go round to gather gifts, we receive our reward.[43]

Such widely known passages in Hellenic philosophy reveal a concept of life as *agon* which suffered sea-changes and outlived its proponents by many centuries.

Evidences of the same idea may be found elsewhere in Greek literature. In tragedy the word ἆθλος was commonly used to designate the suffering of the hero,[44] and ἀθλητής frequently designated the hero (especially Hercules). The word ἀγών, too, was used in tragedy to denote the suffering of the hero (particularly the trials of Hercules).[45] In the treatise *De Spiritu*, sometimes attributed to Aristotle, one finds the word ἀγωνία, which had originally meant "gymnastic exercise," used in the sense of "anguish of mind."[46]

---

[43] *Republic* (621d), trans. Jowett.

[44] Sophocles, *Antigone*, line 856: πατρῷον δ' ἐκτίνεις τιν' ἆθλον. See also ἄθλιος, ἆθλον, and ἆθλος in W. Linwood, *A Lexicon to Aeschylus* (London, 1847), p. 9; F. Ellendt, *Lexicon Sophocleum* (Königsberg, 1835), I, 29; A. Matthias, *Lexicon Euripideum* (Leipzig, 1841), pp. 49ff.; and J. Rumpel, *Lexicon Pindaricum* (Leipzig, 1883), p. 10f.

[45] Sophocles, *Trachiniae*, line 159.

[46] 483a: ἀγωνίαις, rendered "conflict in the soul" by the editor of the

The word ἀγωνιστής itself had an interesting history in Greece. Nearly forty years ago Shorey demonstrated that in fourth-century Athens ἀγωνιστής had become a commonplace in the jargon of educational theory and signified the finished product of education, one fully prepared to take his place in the *agon* of life. The word was used in this sense by the Sophists and especially by Isocrates, the rhetorician whose influence was widespread in the Renaissance.[47] But in Greek literature in general the word ἀγωνιστής usually meant "hero" or "champion," and was often used figuratively, as it was by Plutarch, who referred to Socrates himself as ἀληθείας ἀγωνιστής, "the champion of truth."[48] However, even in the Hellenic period, ἀγωνιστής connoted a certain view of life and of the nature of morality.

The *agon*-idea achieved great prominence in Stoic thought. Professor C. S. Lewis has already shown that what might be

---

Loeb Classics edition. Mr. C. S. Lewis, *Allegory of Love* (Oxford, 1936), p. 58f., however, has argued that Aristotle did not think of moral strength in terms of struggle or conflict. He cites *Ethica Nicomachea*, 1099a and 1104b, and explains that the "really good man, in Aristotle's view, is not tempted"; he is perfect in virtue only when he ceases to feel any tug towards vice. Mr. Lewis treats Aristotle's attitude as typical of the conception of morality held by pagan antiquity and contrasts it with the Stoic and Christian attitude which became predominant in the first century and according to which morality came to be thought of in terms of inner conflict. Mr. Lewis forswears any attempt to account for this change. In my opinion, there is less change to account for than he finds. The spread of the *agon*-concept in pagan antiquity suggests that the same notion of morality as Mr. Lewis calls Christian had been abroad long before the first century; and, if Mr. Lewis is right in denying that Aristotle conceived of morality in terms of conflict in the soul, does not the "change" consist merely in an early and fundamental victory of Platonism over Aristotelianism?

[47] Paul Shorey, "Φύσις, Μελέτη, Ἐπιστήμη," *Transactions and Proceedings of the American Philological Association*, XL (1909), 185-201, esp. 193f. It is of interest in this connection to note that Milton concludes his *Letter to Samuel Hartlib* by asserting that the program of studies which he has described will, "like the last embattelling of a Roman legion," confirm and solidly unite "the whole body of . . . perfected knowledge," and prepare young men "both for peace and war," inspiring them with "a gallant and fearless courage" and with "heroic valour." In this same passage he cites as an authority Isocrates, among others. See Columbia edition, IV, 287f.

[48] *Moralia*, 16c (in *Plutarchi Moralia*, ed. Hubert, Nachstädt, *et al.* [Leipzig, 1925-38], I, 31). Cf. *ibid.*, 561a (*loc.cit.*, III, 426): "[ἡ ψυχὴ] ἀγωνίζεται γὰρ ὥσπερ ἀθλητὴς τὸν βίον," and *ibid.*, 593e (*loc.cit.*, III, 500): "τῶν περὶ τὸν βίον ἀγώνων."

called the morality of conflict "is by no means a result of Christianity, however much Christianity may have done to deepen and perpetuate it."[49] Certain it is, as Mr. Lewis makes plain, that this view of life is strong in the thought of the Stoics. Epictetus constantly taught that "difficulties are what show men's character." He counselled his followers in such words as these:

When a difficult crisis meets you, remember that you are as the raw youth with whom God the trainer is wrestling . . . that you may win at Olympia: and that cannot be done without sweating for it. To my mind no man's difficulties ever gave him a finer trial than yours, if only you will use them for exercise, as the athlete wrestles with the young man.[50]

The strenuousness of virtue is the constant theme of Epictetus. "Life is a soldier's service," says he, and "each man's life is a campaign, and a long and varied one. It is for you to play the soldier's part."[51] The good fight against all sorts of temptation is almost the heart of his philosophy. "When your imagination," he says, "bites deep into your soul, struggle against it with your reason, fight it down, suffer it not to grow strong nor to advance the next step." Wherever you may be stationed, "live a brave life." Zeus may often test you to discover whether you are "a soldier in the true sense,"[52] for, as Seneca also observed, we "must be soldiers, and in a campaign where there is no intermission and no rest."[53] Again, Seneca exhorts us to "conquer all things," all the more because

[49] *Allegory of Love*, p. 59. But, considering the long career of the idea in Greek thought during the previous six centuries, one cannot agree with Mr. Lewis when he implies that the idea originated in the first century, "a characteristic of the whole period from which the Christian empire emerged."

[50] *Discourses*, I, xxiv, trans. P. E. Matheson, in *The Stoic and Epicurean Philosophers: the Complete Extant Writings of Epicurus, Lucretius, Marcus Aurelius* (New York, 1940), p. 264.

[51] *Discourses*, III, xxiv (*loc.cit.*, p. 393).

[52] *Ibid.*, p. 399.

[53] *Epistles*, LI, 6, quoted in Lewis, *op.cit.*, p. 59, n. 4. I am deeply indebted to Mr. Lewis for the support found in his book, without which I should not have perceived the immensely important relevance of Stoic thought in the development of what he terms *psychomachia* and I have here called the *agon*-idea.

"our prize is not a crown nor a palm nor a herald calling silence to cry our name, but virtue, and strength of mind, and peace."[54] For Seneca, as Mr. Lewis rightly maintains, such conflict was the essence of moral life.

So it was, too, for St. Paul, Tertullian, Cyprian, Lactantius, Prudentius, Augustine, Isidore of Seville, and numerous other Christian writers.[55] St. Paul's concept of "the good fight of faith" is but the earliest and best known manifestation of the Christian adoption of this ideal which had originated among the virtuous pagans. Indeed, the agon-idea took its place very close to the heart of Christianity, especially during the period in which the Christian Church was consciously making its way to a spiritual hegemony contra haereticos of whatever coloring. But there is an even more significant respect in which the agon-concept was close to the heart of Christianity.

In an admirable historical study of the Christian doctrine of Atonement, Gustaf Aulén, the Swedish theologian, has pointed out that of all the interpretations of Christ's propitiation of God for the Redemption of Man, only one is ancient enough and persistent enough to be termed "the classical idea of the Atonement." This was not the "subjective" theory, which dates only from the age of the Schoolmen; neither was it the "exemplarist" theory, which developed among the "liberal" theologians of the Enlightenment. The theory which Aulén calls "classical" was first fully formed by Irenaeus,

[54] Epistles, LXXVIII, 16, quoted in Lewis, op.cit., p. 60.

[55] Cf. the long article on agon in the sense of "pugnis spiritalibus, de persecutionibus et martyris" in Thesaurus Linguae Latinae (Leipzig, 1900), I, 1411f. There are many more references to the agon-idea in medieval Christian literature than can be taken into account here. All Christian usage of the words ἀγών, agon, ἀγωνιστής, agonista, ἀθλητής, athleta which I have explored points to the conclusions presented here, where only a sampling of that literature is possible. Cf. Stauffer's article on ἀγών in Theologisches Wörterbuch zum Neuen Testament, ed. G. Kittel (Stuttgart, 1933), I, 134-40. Professor T. S. K. Scott-Craig called my attention to this article of Stauffer's.

One curious use of the word agon may be found in Ambrose (Epist. XIX, 22), who gives the translation "Agon" for the word Lehi in Judges 15:14 and adds that it is so called "to this day" because "ibi Samson gloriosum certamen virtute egregia consummaverit." (Certamen is, of course, a common synonym for agon.)

prevailed during the first ten centuries of the Christian era, was revived by Luther, and remained a central tenet of "orthodox" Protestant theology in the sixteenth and seventeenth centuries. According to this "classical" theory, Christ propitiated God and redeemed Man by struggling against evil, by waging war against the powers of darkness to which Man had been enslaved ever since the Fall. Aulén shows that out of writings in which Christ's mission was expressed in military, athletic, forensic, or dramatic terms arose a conception of *Christus Victor*, who came off triumphantly from his encounter with Satan in the wilderness.[56] My own investigations support Aulén's conclusions. Throughout medieval ecclesiastical literature, the *agon*-idea is found to be completely assimilated by Christianity. Christ is often given the epithet *athleta*, and all the saints come to be written of in similar terms. Among the medieval writers who gave this cast to Christ's victory over Satan were Jerome, Bede, Strabo, Rupert of St. Heribert, and Chrysostom. And in the sixteenth and seventeenth centuries John Knox, Lancelot Andrewes, John Fisher, Franciscus Luca, John Downame, and Thomas Fuller wrote of Christ's encounter with Satan in terms of conflict.[57] This imagery was extended early to all the saints. Am-

---

[56] *Christus Victor: an Historical Study of the Three Main Types of the Idea of the Atonement*, trans. A. G. Hebert (London, 1931), *passim*. An even more exhaustive study of the history of the theory of Christ's Atonement is Elizabeth Marie Pope's *"Paradise Regained": the Tradition and the Poem* (Baltimore, 1947). Professor Pope devotes a section of her final chapter to an examination of the combat images used "whenever the theologians of the Middle Ages or the Renaissance turn to imagery to describe the temptation." As she shows, these writers almost invariably "think and write of it as if it were a struggle between rival warriors or athletes."

[57] Jerome, *Commentarii in Evangelium Matthaei* (*Pat. Lat.*, XXVI, 31); Bede, *In Matthaei Evangelium Expositio* (*Pat. Lat.*, XCII, 18); Strabo, *Expositio in Quatuor Evangelia* (*Pat. Lat.*, CXIV, 870); Rupert of St. Heribert, *In Quatuor Evangelistarum Commentariorum Liber* (*Pat. Lat.*, CLXVII, 1547); Chrysostom, *Homiliae in Matthaeum* (*Pat. Graec.*, LVII, 210); John Knox, *A Notable and Comfortable Exposition of M. John Knoxes, upon the Fourth of Matthew, concerning the Tentation of Christ* (London, 1583), in *Works*, ed. David Laing (Edinburgh, 1856), IV, 103; Lancelot Andrewes, *Seven Sermons on the Wonderful Combat, for God's Glory and Man's Salvation, between Christ and Satan* (first ed. 1592), in *Ninety-six Sermons*, ed. John Parkinson (Oxford, 1841-1843), p. 480; John Fisher, *Analysis Logica Libri S. Lucae* (London, 1597), p. 57; Franciscus Luca,

brose referred to Abraham as "athleta Domini" and to Job
as "athleta fortis Christi [qui] temptationibus eruditus maiore
ad coronam gloria pervenerit."[58] Irenaeus called St. Paul a
"bonus agonista," who summoned all of us to join the struggle (*agonem*) in which he himself was engaged.[59] Isidore of
Seville declared that every saint "se pro agone certaminis
debet offerre."[60] The saint was conceived as continuing Christ's
warfare against the powers of darkness, for, in spite of Christ's
victory over Satan, eternal vigilance was, for every Christian,
the price of Redemption. Theodoret used the verb ἀγωνίζομαι
to mean "struggle in the cause of God after the manner of
saints," and ἀγωνιστής to mean "martyr" or "saint."[61] In
writings attributed to Ignatius of Antioch, one finds Θεοῦ
ἀθλητής, "God's champion," used as an epithet for saints, as
well as for Christ.[62] Countless Christian writers look upon
fortitude as one of the moral virtues,[63] and the pages of our
heritage are peppered with such words as *agon, certamen,
certatio, luctatio, certare, luctari, agonista, certator*, and *athleta*, used almost exclusively in metaphor with spiritual de-
notation.[64] In fact, these words are used so interchangeably
that it is not possible to regard the conceptions of *miles Christianus, athleta Christianus*, and *agonista Christianus* as in any
real sense separate or distinct.

In Lucam Commentaria (first ed. 1606), in *Scripturae Sacrae Cursus Completus*, ed. J. P. Migne (Paris, 1862), XXII, 527; John Downame, *The
Christian Warfare* (London, 1612), p. 15; and Thomas Fuller, *A Comment on the Eleven First Verses of the Fourth Chapter of S. Matthew's
Gospel, concerning Christ's Temptations, delivered in XII Sermons* (London, 1652), pp. 1ff.

[58] *In Psalmos*, XXXVI, lii.

[59] IV, xxxvii, 7.

[60] *Sententiae*, I, xxiii, 3. Cf. Leo Magnus, *Sermo LXXXVII* (*Pat. Lat.*,
LIV).

[61] *Sermo VIII: De Martyribus* (*Pat. Graec.*, LXXXIII, 1032). See also Peter
Chrysologus, *Pat. Lat.*, LII, 497f.: "Datum est illis aliquando discere, dif-
ficilius quidem, sed gloriosius mundo praesente luctari."

[62] *SS. Patrum qui Temporibus Apostolicis Floruerunt . . . Opera*, ed.
J. B. Cotelerius (Amsterdam, 1724), II, 40, 90, 109, 159.

[63] E.g., Tertullian (*Pat. Lat.*, I, 619, 1249); Lactantius (*ibid.*, VI, 595,
625); Augustine, *passim*; Isidore of Seville (*ibid.*, LXXXIII, 1180); Rabanus Maurus (*ibid.*, CX, 1117); Peter Lombard (*ibid.*, CXCII, 822).

[64] Cf. Du Cange, *Glossarium, in loc.*

Nowhere do we find more indicative evidence for the prevalence and development of the *agon*-concept in Christian thought than in the writings of Augustine. He was the author of a treatise entitled *De Agone Christiano*, the thesis of which he expressed in these words: "The crown of victory is vouchsafed only to those who struggle."[65] Here Augustine described Christian life as a holy war, or contest, against evil, a struggle which (waged, as it must be, against what he calls subtle and "prevaricating fallen angels of whom Satan is the chief") would be desperate if Christ had not already, by withstanding the temptation of the most subtle of all the fallen angels, won the all-redeeming victory. But since Christ did triumph, it is a contest the outcome of which is assured if we strive in faith. Augustine expressed the same idea succinctly in the eloquent peroration of his *Sermon 343*:

If we are bowed down with toil, we ask for help. He who appointed the struggle sustains us as we strive. For God does not look down upon your striving as the audience at the games watches the charioteers: they can only cheer; they can be of no help. Not thus does God look upon you as you struggle—not as the champion regards the contender, who can provide but a hay-crown, who cannot strengthen those who are striving to win because he is but a man, not God. And perchance God, from His seat on high, labors more than those who struggle in the arena here. For when God looks down upon His champions, He sustains them if they call upon Him; and, indeed, the voice of His own Champion is heard in the Psalm: *When I said, My foot slippeth; thy mercy, O Lord, held me up.* Therefore let us not be slothful, my brothers: let us strive, let us seek, let us strike. *For everyone that asketh receiveth; and he that seeketh findeth; and to him that knocketh it shall be opened.*[66]

[65] "Corona victoriae non promittitur nisi certantibus" (*Corp. Script. Eccles. Lat.*, XLI, 101-38). The *De Agone Christiano* was first printed at Basel in 1506.

[66] "Si in labore subdeficimus, adjutorium imploremus. Adjuvat certantem qui certamen indixit. Non enim sic te Deus exspectat certantem, ut populus aurigam: clamare novit, adjuvare non novit. Non sic te Deus exspectat certantem, ut agonista exspectat athletam: coronam feneam parat, vires subministrare laboranti non novit; nec enim potest, homo enim est, non Deus. Et forte dum exspectat, plus laborat sedendo, quam ille luctando. Nam Deus quando exspectat certatores suos, adjuvat eos invocatus: nam

Thus it can be seen that the epithet *Agonistes* in the title of Milton's tragedy connotes much that is close to the heart of the Christian tradition. Milton himself in the *Christian Doctrine* (I, xxi) referred explicitly to St. Paul's strictures on "the good fight of faith" in the Epistles to Timothy and urged all Christians to strive after perfection with earnestness, pointing out that even in the regenerate there is necessarily a continuing struggle between the flesh and the spirit and a warfare against the dominion of Satan.[67] This is a view of Christian life characteristic of Protestant orthodoxy in the seventeenth century, and particularly characteristic of Milton himself. In the *Second Defense* he spoke of himself as having "come off victorious in the noblest far of all contests," that is, in striving after virtue and truth.[68] And every reader of Milton remembers the noble passage of *Areopagitica* in which the life of the true Christian ("the true, warfaring Christian," as apparently he said elsewhere) is likened to a race where the "immortal garland" of virtue must be "run for, not without dust and heat." This idea, which Milton inherited from ages past, is implicit in the struggle between good and evil in *Paradise Lost* and in the contest between Christ and Satan in *Paradise Regained*. In *Samson Agonistes* the Chorus sings in thanksgiving for the "invincible might" of Samson, "the deliverer" sent by God

> To quell the mighty of the Earth, th' oppressour,
> The brute and boist'rous force of violent men . . .
> With plain Heroic magnitude of mind
> And celestial vigour arm'd. (1272-80)

But the full significance of the Christian idea of the *agon* in *Samson Agonistes* can be appreciated only when we have considered the difficult question of the relevance of the allegorical interpretation of Samson to Milton's tragedy.

---

ejus athletae vox est in Psalmo. . . . Non ergo simus pigri, fratres mei: petamus, quaeramus, pulsemus" (*Pat. Lat.*, XXXIX, 1511).

[67] Columbia edition, XVI, 18f.

[68] Columbia edition, VIII, 192f. In *Doctrine and Discipline of Divorce* (Columbia edition, III, 419) Milton used *agony* and *strife* as synonyms.

5

WHEN *Samson Agonistes* was printed in 1671, the allegorical interpretation of Samson, which had always been a prominent feature of the tradition, still persisted in nearly all the commentaries, sermons, contemplations, and literary allusions to Samson.[69] James Calfhill, in *An Answer to John Martiall's Treatise of the Cross* (1565), made Samson's victory with the jawbone an allegorical figure of "how Christ . . . hath overthrown the adversary Power; hath by one death destroyed all the enemies of life."[70] In *A Briefe of the Bible* (1596), Henoch Clapham said of Samson, "A Nazarite hee was, and a figure of our Nazaret Anointed."[71] Thomas Hayne's tabular representation of many of the parallels between Samson and Christ was set forth in the *General View of the Holy Scriptures* (1607, 1614, 1640). Among these parallels was the following:

The Philistines having *Sampson* in Azza a strong Citie, shut the gates upon him, thought there to hold him fast, and to prevail over him; but hee carried away the gates of the Citie, and frustrated their plot.	The Jews, and Romans haveing *Christ* in his grave a strong prison house, had him shut up with a grave stone sealed, and kept with a watch, and thought there to hold him fast: but he conquered death and the grave, and rose again to life, never to die more.[72]

George Herbert found in the Samson story a simile of Redemption which depends upon allegorical interpretation:

> The rest of our Creation
> Our great Redeemer did remove
> With the same shake, which at his passion
> Did th' earth and all things with it move.
> As Sampson bore the doores away,
> Christs hands, though nail'd, wrought our salvation,
> And did unhinge that day.[73]

[69] See above, p. 68f., and n. 9.
[70] Ed. Richard Gibbings, "Parker Society Publications" (Cambridge, 1846), p. 336.
[71] P. 68f.   [72] P. 218.
[73] "Sunday," lines 43-49, in *Works*, ed. F. E. Hutchinson (Oxford, 1941), p. 76.

In his *Annotationes in Biblia* (1607),[74] John Diodati, a thoroughgoing Calvinist, interpreted Samson entirely in allegorical terms, treating even Samson's visit to the harlot (Judges 16:3) as "a figure of Christ his glorious Resurrection, who could not be detained by death."[75] And such a thesaurus of all exegesis as Matthew Poole's *Synopsis Criticorum* (1669-1676) displayed the allegorical comments of most of the great Christian writers up to that time, the very day of the publication of *Samson Agonistes*. There can be no doubt but that the allegorical interpretation of Samson as a figure of Christ was, in the seventeenth century, one of the most prevalent connotations of the hero of Milton's tragedy. It is impossible to suppose that any of Milton's literate contemporaries could have thought of Samson without thinking also of Christ.

And yet in *Samson Agonistes* one finds almost no vestige of this aspect of the tradition. There is but one shred of palpable internal evidence to suggest that Milton intended the poem to call to mind the age-old correspondence between Samson and Christ. Near the opening of the poem the Chorus recalls, with painful contrast, the former glorious deeds of the hero:

> Then with what trivial weapon came to hand,
> The Jaw of a dead Ass, his sword of bone,
> A thousand fore-skins fell, the flower of *Palestin*
> In *Ramath-lechi* famous to this day. (142-45)

Again when Samson himself remembers his past exploits, he boasts:

> On thir whole Host I flew
> Unarm'd, and with a trivial weapon fell'd
> Their choicest youth; they only liv'd who fled. (262-64)

A similar reference to Samson's only weapon may be found in Francis Quarles' *Historie of Samson*:

> The jaw-bone of an Asse? How poore a thing
> God makes his powerful instrument to bring

[74] English trans., *Pious and Learned Annotations upon the Holy Bible*, 1648; fourth ed. 1664.
[75] *In loc.*, Judges 16:3.

Some honour to his name, and to advance
His greater glory![76]

All three of these passages reflect one of the persistent features of the Samson tradition, a feature often associated with allegorical interpretation. Christian writers who dealt with Samson, whether in annotation, homily, or poem, devoted a good deal of space to the jawbone with which he slew a thousand Philistines. Ambrose remarked that, because he was strengthened by the Holy Spirit, "the victorious Samson was so indomitable that he could slay thousands of men with only the jawbone of an ass." Then he referred to Matthew 5:39 and the doctrine: "Whosoever shall smite thee on thy right cheek, turn to him the other also."[77] Gregory the Great seems to have been the first to give an explicitly allegorical interpretation of the jawbone. It was, said he, a prefiguring of "Redemptor enim noster simplicitatem atque patientiam praedicantium suae manu virtutis tenens."[78] This is the sort of paradox which has always been of the very essence of Christianity, and this allegorical parallel was repeated by many subsequent commentators. Strabo cited Gregory as his authority for stating that Samson's jawbone signifies the Gospel of Christ, especially the "simplicity and sufferance" which characterized Christ's teaching.[79] In the ninth century, Rabanus Maurus perpetuated this allegory, repeating the exact words used earlier by Gregory.[80] Peter Damiani, in the eleventh century, wrote a sermon on I Corinthians 1:19: "For it is written, I will destroy the wisdom of the wise, and will bring to nothing the understanding of the prudent. . . . Hath not God made foolish the wisdom of this world?" He stressed

---

[76] "Meditation VIII," in *Complete Works*, ed. A. B. Grosart (Edinburgh, 1880-1881), II, 160.

[77] *De Spiritu Sancto*, xii (*Pat. Lat.*, XVI, 775).

[78] In Paterius, *Liber de Expositione Veteris ac Novi Testamenti, de Diversis Libris S. Gregorii Magni Concinnatus*, VI, v (*Pat. Lat.*, LXXIX, 789).

[79] *Glossa Ordinaria, in loc.* Judges 15:16 (*Pat. Lat.*, CXIII, 532). This gloss was reprinted in Nicholas de Lyra's *Biblia Sacra* (London, 1545), *in loc.*

[80] *In Librum Judicum et Ruth*, xviii (*Pat. Lat.*, CVIII, 1191).

the homely simplicity of the Gospel of Christ and appealed
again to the example of Samson's victory with the jawbone,
which, he said, prefigured the triumph of simple Christian
truth over ancient error.[81] And in Milton's own century John
Diodati contrived even more allegory for the episode of the
jawbone: Samson's thirst after this battle with the Philistines
in Ramath-lechi was, he thought, a figure of "the spiritual
heat" of Christ in all His combats, but especially of His thirst
on the Cross.[82] Even so minute a feature of Samson's story
was capable of bearing immense Christian significance when
the methods of allegory were applied. Milton's phrase, "triv-
ial weapon," could hardly have failed to bring such larger
meanings as those just reviewed to the mind of a seventeenth-
century reader, and Milton himself could scarcely have been
unaware that the phrase would have such connotations for his
reader.

To be sure, one looks in vain for more tangible internal evidence of allegorical interpretation in *Samson Agonistes*, although there are passages in which one whose ear is attuned
to the tradition can hear echoes of the many allegorical analogies between Samson and Christ. Samson's account of Dalila's
attempts to wring from him the secret of his strength is but
one of these. Samson tells (lines 392-407) how "thrice she
assay'd with flattering prayers and sighs" to win his secret,
and how he "deluded her" at first and turned her importunity
to sport. To the seventeenth-century reader, soaked in a tradition according to which all the heroes of the Old Testament
were considered to be figurative foreshadowings of the Christian Story, and especially to such a reader coming fresh from

[81] *Collectanea in Vetus Testamentum: in Librum Judicum*, xii (*Pat. Lat.*,
CXLV, 1089f.). See also Damiani's *Sermo LXVIII* (*ibid.*, CXLIV, 892f.).
Rupert of St. Heribert, *In Librum Judicum*, xix (*ibid.*, CLXVII, 1041-55),
repeated this allegory of the jawbone. In spite of the breadth and depth of
his own learning, Milton often expressed opinions which are anti-intellec-
tual, or perhaps more exactly, super-intellectual. The expressions of these
opinions—one of the most striking of which is that assigned to Christ in
Paradise Regained, IV, 291-330—agree well with I Corinthians 1:19 and
with the conception of the Gospel set forth in all these allegorical interpretations of the jawbone.
[82] *Pious and Learned Annotations, in loc.* Judges 15:18.

the vivid portrayal of Satan's temptations of Christ in *Paradise Regained*, Samson was not simply Samson here, nor Dalila simply Dalila.[83]

When one considers the *actualité* of the allegorized Samson in the seventeenth century, and when one acknowledges the fact that Milton made no alterations in the story which might have counteracted the reader's tendency to perceive Christ in Samson, one must conclude that the poet expected the reader himself to bring this much to the poem. Could a reader in Milton's time have failed to respond to both the implied comparison and the implied contrast of Christ and Samson? If, as the external evidence overwhelmingly indicates, he could not, then must we not admit the strong probability that this allegorical duality was part of—perhaps even the center of— the meaning which the poet intended the tragedy to have?

Reluctant as one may be to grant that Milton made use of allegory—especially in *Samson Agonistes*—this appears to be an inescapable conclusion. It must, of course, be borne in mind that this is not allegory in the usual, or merely poetic, sense; it is allegory in the technical, exegetical sense, by which is meant the assumption that Samson and his story are a figure of Christ and His story. Nor have we any reason to believe that Milton himself disdained allegory, even of a more general kind, on either artistic or doctrinal grounds. He had little need of allegory in *Paradise Lost* and *Paradise Regained*, for even the literal meaning of those poems is on the anagogical level. Where he could make good use of allegory—as in the episode of Sin and Death in *Paradise Lost*—he did so, apparently without compunction. Each of the stairs to Heaven was allegorically significant, as Milton tells us in *Paradise Lost*, III, 516. *Comus* is, of course, entirely allegorical. Moreover, Milton readily accepted the allegorical interpretation of Ariosto, Tasso, and Spenser, in which, as he said, "more is

[83] Note the verbal parallels in the account of Dalila's temptation of Samson in Judges, in the recounting of Satan's speechlessness (*Paradise Lost*, I, 619), and in *Samson Agonistes*, lines 392-407.

meant than meets the ear."[84] Nor did he think less of those
poets for that: could Spenser otherwise be reckoned "a better
teacher than Scotus or Aquinas"? In matters of biblical exegesis Milton's attitude towards allegory was not unfavorable.
At one point in the *Christian Doctrine*[85] he opened a discussion
by admitting that perhaps an allegorical interpretation of
Scripture should not be made the basis of an argument on a
much-disputed question; but then he went on to use allegory
to the full in that very argument. Elsewhere in the same
work, in the midst of a discussion of the Covenant of Grace,
Milton made free use of allegorical exegesis, saying that
Moses prefigured Christ's Redemption of Man both in liberating the Israelites from Egyptian bondage and also in the
brazen serpent, a symbol of expiation and redemption. Such
elements of the Old Testament story, said Milton, "serve
unto the example and shadow of heavenly things."[86] In *The
Likeliest Means to Remove Hirelings out of the Church*, Milton remarked that Melchisedec was "incited . . . by the secret
providence of God, intending him for a type of Christ and
his priesthood."[87] And of Revelations Milton said, "The
whole Booke soars to a Prophetic pitch in types and Allegories."[88]

6

IN THE very title of this tragedy Milton invited his readers
to think of Samson as a model of virtue, as a hero, as a champion of God, as a saint, a martyr, and a counterpart of Christ.
For Milton accords to Samson the epithet used for other
saints and even for Christ. Peter Abelard had called Samson
"athleta nobilis"; Milton's use of *Agonistes* gives us, when
we consider the complex significance of the term, ample reason to conclude that he regarded Samson as Θεοῦ ἀθλητής,
as an exemplification of the highest pitch to which Man can
rise.

[84] "Il Penseroso," line 120.   [85] Columbia edition, XIV, 93.
[86] *Ibid.*, XVI, 103.   [87] *Ibid.*, VI, 55.
[88] *Animadversions upon the Remonstrants Defence*, xiii (*ibid.*, III, 154).

But this is not yet all that allegory and the title, when taken together, reveal.

As Dr. Pope has shown, the temptations both of Adam (through Eve) in Paradise and of Christ (through Satan) in the wilderness were the subject of much subtle theorizing in the Middle Ages and the Reformation.[89] By the time of Milton, the distinctions among the several principal kinds of temptation were fully and clearly developed. Seventeenth-century theologians conceived of three separate temptations: (1) *concupiscentia carnis*, sometimes represented by gluttony alone, and figuratively designated as "the flesh"; (2) *concupiscentia oculorum*, or vainglory, known figuratively as "the world"; and (3) *superbia vitae*, originally comprising only avarice, figuratively "the Devil." In Protestant theology, *concupiscentia carnis* had come to be thought of as temptation by necessity; *concupiscentia oculorum*, as temptation by fraud (or persuasion); *superbia vitae*, as temptation by violence (or fear).[90] According to this scheme, Satan had tempted Man in Paradise (1) by necessity, when he argued that the fruit was edible and needed as food; (2) by fraud when he used flattery and when he lied about the results which would follow upon the eating; and (3) by violence or fear when he spoke threateningly of death and represented the forbidden fruit as a means of attaining God-like deathlessness. Satan's temptation of Christ in the wilderness was analyzed according to this same scheme: (1) the temptation to turn stones into bread was necessity; (2) the temptation of the kingdoms was fraud; and (3) the temptation of the tower was violence or fear.

This "triple equation," as Dr. Pope calls it, gives us a clue to the larger meaning of *Samson Agonistes*, if we are willing to follow the implications of the title and of the correspondence between Samson and Christ afforded by allegorical interpretation. It leads us again to ground on which we can dismiss Dr. Johnson's complaint against the dramatic structure of Milton's tragedy.

In Milton's poem Samson is visited by three principal

[89] *Op.cit.*, esp. ch. v.   [90] *Ibid.*, p. 53.

agents, each of whom can be regarded as exemplifying one of the three temptations just defined. Manoa, the first of these agents, tempts Samson to forsake his vocation as ἀγωνιστής by offering him liberty, ease, and peace in retirement. He has, he says, "made way" already in a plan to ransom his son from the Philistines. Manoa (lines 502-20) argues against too rigorous an adherence to a conception of duty and concludes:

> Reject not then what offerd means, who knows
> But God hath set before us, to return thee
> Home to thy countrey.

Manoa is not a deceiver, at least not consciously. He urges on Samson a choice which he believes to be necessary. Samson is blind and weak and helpless; he can, in Manoa's view, do no more now in the cause of God; in spite of his previous shortcomings, he has earned retirement as champion *emeritus*. This is the *concupiscentia carnis*, "the flesh," the temptation by necessity. And the temptation is directed against Samson's faith in his God. The implication of Manoa's plea is that God allowed Samson to fail, abandoned His champion; it is primarily for this reason that he would be justified now in retiring and ministering to his own personal needs. Manoa relies on what Man can do without divine aid; he hopes to come to terms with the Philistines. Though Samson refuses the hope which his father holds out to him, he is not unmoved by the temptation to acquiesce in merely human means for the achievement of merely human ends. He agrees that his mission now looks hopeless, and he admits that he is now so dispirited that

> nature within me seems
> In all her functions weary of herself;
> My race of glory run, and race of shame,
> And I shall shortly be with them that rest. (595-98)

He acknowledges an even more compelling feeling of the necessity of complying with Manoa's plea than mere weariness of the flesh: he suffers, he says (606-16), from a spiritual fatigue, a malady that has pierced his "inmost mind." His last words to Manoa are not a very positive rebuff; he has reached, at the end of this interview, only a resolution of despair. Manoa's temptation fails only because Samson is convinced that his ills are not such as home and the kindly ministry of his father can cure.

> This one prayer yet remains, might I be heard,
> No long petition, speedy death,
> The close of all my miseries, and the balm. (649-51)

It is in this utter hopelessness that Samson is confronted next by Dalila, the "specious monster," the fraudulent one. It is she, more than either Manoa or Harapha, who uses arguments, who tries to *persuade* Samson. She, like Manoa, has a conception of the good life which is essentially different from Samson's. She, too, thinks in human terms alone. She is concerned with the little loves and hatreds of mankind, with jealousies, with caresses, with the matters of every day. With all her finery on, she is rosy-cheeked, clear-eyed, and untouched by any of life's deeper or more troubling thoughts or feelings; she is equally unmoved by any such high aspirations as have ruled Samson prior to his fall and since the beginning of his repentance. She is precisely the kind of person to make one who is devoted to a high calling doubtful of the wisdom of following the star. Like Manoa, she tempts Samson to forsake his faith, but she does so by means of fraud and persuasion. She seeks to convince Samson (lines 766-818) that she was compelled to betray him by such weaknesses as are characteristic of all mortals, by feminine curiosity, and by a jealous love for him so overpowering that she wanted only to make him her prisoner in luxurious captivity; she wants him to believe that she has sorely repented for the ills which she unwittingly occasioned. She asks him to remember that he is more inflexible than other poor human beings, that she is no superwoman. When he scorns these arguments, she has more. She claims (lines 843-70) that she yielded to the satraps only after they girt her round with sieges and persuaded her that she owed that service to her nation and her god. But Samson sees through all her rhetoric; he is now immune to her

"circling wiles," and he recognizes her defense of herself by
"feign'd Religion" to be "smooth hypocrisie." Finally she
uses the most powerful instrument of rhetoric: the appeal to
the emotions. She abases herself completely (lines 907-27),
begs Samson to forgive her for her foolishness and rashness,
and pleads for a chance to redeem herself by procuring his
freedom and caring for him, even as Manoa had offered to
do. When this last resource fails, she gives herself away entirely (lines 960-96); she rages and storms in such a way as
to leave no doubt that all her previous arguments were fraudulent, that she is, as the Chorus remarks,

> a manifest Serpent by her sting
> Discover'd in the end, till now conceal'd.

She, too, makes her temptation felt, even though Samson re-
sists her rhetoric and her wiles. After she has gone, he reveals
(lines 999-1002) that he is now plunged even more deeply
into hopelessness, for she has reminded him of the grossness
of his sin in foolishly revealing his "sacred trust" to such a
deceiver as she. Her trial of his faith by the temptation of
fraudulent persuasion has not succeeded, but Samson has not
yet found any resolution of his own conviction of failure in a
sacred vocation.[91]

Harapha finds Samson at this depth of despair, and he
plagues Samson finally with the temptation of "the Devil."
Satan, as a last resort, had carried Christ to the topmost pin-
nacle of the temple, where, as the Son of Man, Christ was
in real jeopardy. There Satan challenged him to make a test
of his Father's care for him by throwing himself to the earth
below. The implication was that God might have abandoned
Christ. It was in this last respect that the temptation of the
tower was implemented by fear as well as by violence. It was,
moreover, addressed to Christ's faith: Satan wished to suggest
that God had deserted His champion. Here Harapha bears
the same relation to Samson as Satan bore to Christ in the

[91] It must not be forgotten that Dalila, as traitress, had already been
likened to Judas. Cf. Jacobus Bonfrerius, *In Ioshuam, Iudices, et Ruth*
(Paris, 1631), p. 377, col. 2.

final temptation; Harapha represents the temptation by violence and fear. His temptation by violence is rather subtle: he is so ready with foul insults and so completely a thing of mere brutal force that Samson is tempted to fall back upon brutal force alone to rid himself of this gadfly, is sufficiently moved by the temptation to be willing to meet Harapha in mortal combat. The temptation by violence alone, however, has not touched Samson's central characteristic; he is ready to engage in mortal combat with Harapha because his "trust . . . in the living God" is still strong. For this reason Harapha shifts to another ground:

> Presume not on thy God, what e're he be,
> Thee he regards not, owns not, hath cut off
> Quite from his people, and delivered up
> Into thy Enemies hand. (1156-59)

This temptation—precisely equivalent to Satan's final trial of Christ, as it was conceived by Christian commentators—is the most galling of all for Samson. It is designed to call up the fear that he has been abandoned by his God. This is the utmost temptation of "the Devil," the most potent weapon the powers of darkness have at their disposal. But Samson somehow finds his faith still proof against temptation. He cannot deny that he has sunk to the lowest depths of thralldom and humiliation, but he devoutly believes that "these indignities" were inflicted justly by his God, and he still does not despair at least of God's "final pardon."

Critics of *Samson Agonistes* have long wondered what suggested to Milton that he invent Harapha and introduce him in this tragedy. It is true, as many have said, that he serves as a foil for Samson; and it could be, as Professor Boughner has suggested, that he comes out of the Italian comedies. But he is not a comic agent in *Samson Agonistes*, and a character in drama seldom functions solely as a foil. Harapha is more organic in the plot of *Samson Agonistes* than either of these theories would make him. He is demanded by the very material with which the poet was working. He is demanded by

the "triple equation" of temptation, for he is the instrument
of temptation by violence and fear. He is demanded by the
agon-concept, for the existence of an agonist implies the existence of an antagonist. He is demanded by the allegorical tradition: he stands in relation to Samson as Satan to Christ. Even
the ancient correspondence of Samson and Hercules requires
for Samson a figure equivalent to Hercules' Antaeus, who
was also a giant. Milton had already (*Paradise Regained*, IV,
563-71) compared Christ in conflict with Satan to Hercules
in conflict with Antaeus.[92] In *Samson Agonistes* the double
proportion, as well as the triple equation, is complete: Antaeus is to Hercules, as Satan to Christ, as Harapha to Samson. And when one remembers that Satan was conceived, too,
as the Adversary of Man, one begins to comprehend the mul-
tiplicity of connotations which *Samson Agonistes* had for the
reader whom Milton addressed.[93]

From the time of the writing of the Epistle to the Hebrews,
Samson had been known, above all, as an exemplar of faith.
It was for this distinction that he was named in that document

[92] The correspondence between Hercules and Christ had been developed
in the Renaissance by Jacobus Bonus in his *De Vita & Gestis Christi eiusque
Mysteriis & Documentis Opus Egregium . . . Carmine Heroico Eleganter ac
Mirifice Congestum . . . : Eiusdem Iacobi Praeludium in Treis Distinctum
Libros, trium Gratiarum Nominibus Appellatos, atque Herculis Labores
& Gesta in Christi Figuram* (Rome, 1526). It is also well to recall here
that Augustine had made Samson's death in the temple a figure of our
Redemption by Christ. See *Sermo CCCLXIV* (*Pat. Lat.*, XXXIX, 1643).

[93] Milton used Harapha for another purpose too. He is a means of
introducing ideas about Samson with which Milton disagreed, ideas suggested by commentators whom Milton distrusted. Milton was especially
likely to differ with the later medieval commentators, with the Schoolmen.
Rupert of St. Heribert, the only commentator who ever called Samson's
sainthood into question, had suggested (*Pat. Lat.*, CLXVII, 1050) that perhaps Samson wrought his wondrous feats by means of magic, that is, by
alliance with Satan rather than by impulsion of the Holy Spirit. In *Samson
Agonistes* (lines 1130-38) Harapha makes the same charge, and Samson
replies:

I know no Spells, use no forbidden Arts;
My trust is in the living God who gave me
At my Nativity this strength. (1139-41)

Harapha's imputation that Samson is just an outlaw (lines 1185-88) likewise creates an occasion for the hero to reply to commentators who regarded
him as an unauthorized privateer.

among the saints of the Old Testament. It was on that ground that he was first adopted as a saint by Christianity. *Samson Agonistes* takes up this ancient theme; it deals with Samson's struggle to preserve his faith against all the temptations by which Man may be tried. His father represents the demands of necessity, tempting Samson to relinquish his faith in God and his vocation as God's champion by succumbing to the ways of "the flesh" and accepting the ease of retirement. Dalila—bedecked with the signs of prosperity granted to those who follow the way of "the world"—represents the insidiousness of fraudulent persuasion; she, too, sorely tries a dedicated spirit's devotion to a high purpose, in part by asserting that she, too, had been serving her god and her nation. When the appeal to human need and the resources of fraudulent rhetoric have failed, Samson is pitted at last against the temptation by violence and fear in the person of Harapha. This last temptation is also aimed at undermining his faith, for Harapha implies that Samson's God has forgotten him. In connection with each of these temptations, it is on Samson's faith that emphasis is placed. His sea of faith is at its lowest ebb during and immediately after the interview with Manoa; then he despairs of everything but the chance that God will grant him "speedy death." In spite of the challenges of Dalila and Harapha, his faith is kept whole. When Harapha has done his worst, Samson still trusts in God's "final pardon." Is it not in these three trials of faith that the "middle" of the tragedy is to be found? If the triumph of faith is, as the tradition indicates, the center of Samson's story, is not that part of the tragedy in which that victory hangs balanced in doubt the "middle" of the plot? Aristotle defined the "middle" as "that which naturally comes after something else and is followed by a third thing." Samson's ordeal of faith comes after his fall from glorious Nazariteship and as a result of it, and it is followed by his ultimate victory in the temple of Dagon. Nor is the catastrophe merely *post hoc*. Samson can rally himself to this final service of God only because his faith in God has been kept through vicissitude and tempered in the fire of temptation. His ending has a perfect *propter hoc* connection with those temptations.

7

WHEN the modern reader reconsiders *Samson Agonistes* in the light shed by even so faltering an attempt as this to kindle the long-unused lamps of a lost tradition, he is led to conclude that there must be a vast disparity between what the poem could have meant to Milton and what it has meant to most of Milton's critics. We have too often read the poem as if it were a nineteenth- or a twentieth-century work.

Perhaps for this reason we have heretofore made too much of what Verity called "a minor key of sad resignation" in the poem. Samson, it is true, must sacrifice himself in his ultimate fulfillment of the mission for which he was promised, and it is in that human sense that the meaning of the poem is tragic. But this is a special sort of tragedy, not just a re-creation of the tragedy of the Greeks, however perfect it may be in that respect. It is a tragedy, and in the Greek acceptation of that term, in form as well as in human meaning; but it is a Greek tragedy written by an unyielding Christian poet living in England when the tradition of Christianity was seventeen hundred years old. For this reason we may not ignore the fact that Samson is finally victorious over God's enemies because he withstands temptation.

Samson stands for more than the victorious Nazarite, the faithful champion of God. He brings to full circle the immense story which Milton took up in *Paradise Lost* and continued in *Paradise Regained*. In Eden Man was tempted, succumbed to temptation, and fell from grace. In the wilderness Christ, in the rôle of the Redeemer, atoned for Man's sin and restored him to grace by winning against Satan the victory which alone makes all victory possible. But *Paradise Regained* did not complete the cycle. There Christ took on the flesh and appeared as the Son of Man, but he acted in the person of the Son of God, an aspect of the Divine. It was left to demonstrate the victory on the human level. Samson's story, paralleling as it does the story of *Christus Victor*, reveals him as *Homo Victor*, a palpable exemplification of the meaning to Man of his Redemption. His victory is possible to all who keep the faith. The *agon* against evil and its temptations, in whatever form, is Man's vocation. And in a state of grace he can be confident of ultimate triumph.

The final Chorus of *Samson Agonistes*, like all the rest of the poem, must be read before the colossal backdrop of the whole scheme of Fall and Redemption. Only *Samson Agonistes* shows at last that

> All is best, though we oft doubt,
> What th' unsearchable dispose
> Of highest wisdom brings about,
> And ever best found in the close.

Only if we read his tragedy in the light of the Christian tradition can we see in it the fulfillment, not only of Milton's early intention "to sing the victorious agonies of martyrs and saints," but also of his larger ambition to

> assert Eternal Providence,
> And justifie the wayes of God to men.

Few poets—indeed, few men of any sort—have ever achieved so fully an exalted purpose. *Samson Agonistes* is, in more ways than we have sometimes understood, the close of a dedicated life.

Bibliography

I. PRIMARY SOURCES

THE first item listed here is the general reference work used as a source of the writings of most of the Church Fathers and Schoolmen. This work is subsequently referred to in the Bibliography as *Patrologia latina* and *Patrologia graeca*:

Migne, J. P., ed. Patrologiae cursus completus; seu, bibliotheca universalis, integra, uniformis, commoda, oeconomica, omnium SS. patrum, doctorum scriptorumque ecclesiasticorum, sive latinorum, sive graecorum, qui ab aevo apostolico ad tempora Innocenti III, (ann 1216) pro latinis et ad Concilii florentini tempora (ann 1439) pro graecis floruerunt. . . . Series graecae, Paris, 1857-1903. . . . Series latine, Paris, 1844-1903.

Abelard, Peter. Planctus varii. Patrologia latina, CLXXVIII.

Ælfric. The homilies of the Anglo-Saxon church. Ed. Benjamin Thorpe. London, 1844-1846. 2 vols.

———. The Old English version of the Heptateuch. Ed. S. J. Crawford. EETS, original series, no. 160. London, 1922.

Alanus ab Insulis. De fide catholica contra haereticos. Patrologia latina, CCX.

———. Sermones octo. Patrologia latina, CCX.

Ambrose. Apologia altera prophetae David. Patrologia latina, XIV.

———. De spiritu sancto. Patrologia latina, XVI.

———. Epistola XIX. Patrologia latina, XVI.

———. Expositio in septem visiones libri Apocalypsis. Patrologia latina, XVII.

Andrewes, Lancelot. Ninety-six sermons. Ed. John Parkinson. Oxford, 1841-1843. 2 vols. Vol. 1.

Aristotle. De arte poetica. Ed. Ingram Bywater. Oxford, 1911.

———. De poetica. Trans. Ingram Bywater. In the basic works of Aristotle. Ed. Richard McKeon. New York, 1941.

———. On the art of poetry. Trans. and amplified by Lane Cooper. New York, 1913.

Athanasius. Ad episcopos Ægyptii et Libyae epistola encyclica contra Arianos. Patrologia graeca, XXV.

Atto of Vercelli. Expositio in epistolas S. Pauli: epistola ad Hebraeos. Patrologia latina, CXXXIV.

Augustine. Contra Faustium libri XXXIII. Ed. J. Zycha. Corpus scriptorum ecclesiasticorum latinorum, XXV. Vienna, 1891.

Augustine. Contra Gaudentium donatistarum episcopum libri II.
Patrologia latina, XLIII.
―――. De agone christiano. Ed. J. Zycha. Corpus scriptorum
ecclesiasticorum latinorum, XLI. Vienna, 1900.
―――. De civitate Dei contra paganos. Patrologia latina, XLI.
―――. De opere monachorum. Ed. J. Zycha. Corpus scrip-
torum ecclesiasticorum latinorum, XLI. Vienna, 1900.
―――. Enarrationes in Psalmos. Patrologia latina, XXXVII.
―――. Locutionum in Heptateuchum libri VII. Ed. J. Zycha.
Corpus scriptorum ecclesiasticorum latinorum, XXVIII. Vienna,
1894.
―――. Quaestionum in Heptateuchum libri VII. Ed. J. Zycha.
Corpus scriptorum ecclesiasticorum latinorum, XXVIII. Vienna,
1895.
―――. Sermo CCCXLIII. Patrologia latina, XXXIX.
―――. Sermo CCCLXIV. Patrologia latina, XXXIX.
―――. Sermo de tempore barbarico. Patrologia latina, XL.
Bede Venerabilis. In Matthaei evangelium expositio. Patrologia
latina, XCII.
―――. Quaestiones super librum Judicum. Patrologia latina,
XCIII.
Bible. Biblia, the Bible, that is, the Holy Scripture of the olde and
new Testament, faithfully and truly translated in to Englische
(1535). Trans. Miles Coverdale. London, 1838.
―――. Biblia maxima. Ed. Jean de la Haye. Paris, 1660. Vol.
IV.
―――. Biblia sacra cum glossis. Ed. Nicholas de Lyra. London,
1545. Vol. II.
―――. The Bible, that is, the Holy Scripture conteined in the
old and new Testament. Translated according to the Ebrew
and Greeke, and conferred with the best translations in divers
languages. With most profitable annotations upon all hard
places, and other things of great importance. London, 1599.
First edition, 1560; the so-called "Breeches" Bible.
―――. The hexaglot Bible. Ed. Edward Riches de Levante,
et al. London, 1874. 6 vols.
―――. The Holy Bible, containing the old and new Testaments
with the apocryphal books, in the earliest English versions made
from the Latin Vulgate by John Wycliffe and his followers.
Ed. J. Forshall and F. Madden. Oxford, 1850. 4 vols.
―――. The Holy Bible translated from the Latin Vulgate diligently compared with the Hebrew, Greek, and other editions
in divers languages. The old Testament first published by the

English college at Douay, A.D. 1609 and the new Testament
first published by the English college at Rheims, A.D. 1582.
Baltimore and New York, 1899.

———. Testamenti veteris Biblia sacra sive libri canonici, priscae
Iudaeorum ecclesiae a Deo traditi, latini recens ex Hebraeo
facti, brevibusque scholiis illustrati ab Immanuele Tremellio &
Francisco Iunio: accesserunt libri qui vulgo dicuntur apocryphi,
latine redditi & notis quibusdam aucti a Francisco Iunio. London, 1580. First edition, 1579.

Bonfrerius, Jacobus. Commentarii in Ioshuam, Iudices, et Ruth.
Paris, 1631.

Bonus, Jacobus. De vita & gestis Christi eiusque mysteriis & documentis opus egregium . . . carmine heroico eleganter ac mirifice
congestum. . . . Eiusdem Iacobi praeludium in treis distinctum
libros, trium gratiarum nominibus appellatos, atque Herculis
labores & gesta in Christi figuram. Mystice ac pulcherrime eodem
carmine continentes. Rome, 1526.

Brenz, Johann. In librum Iudicum et Ruth commentarius. The
Hague, 1535.

Bullinger, Henry. The decades. Trans. H. I. Ed. Thomas Harding. Parker society publications. Cambridge, 1850.

Burton, Robert. The anatomy of melancholy. Ed. A. R. Shilleto.
London, 1893. 3 vols.

Cajetan (Tommaso de Vio Gaetano). Opera omnia in S. Scripturam. London, 1637. Vol. II.

Calfhill, James. An answer to John Martiall's treatise of the cross.
Ed. Richard Gibbings. Parker society publications. Cambridge,
1846.

Calvin, Jean. Commentaries on the epistle of Paul the Apostle.
Trans. John Owen. Calvin translation society. Edinburgh,
1853.

Caxton, William. Mirrour of the world. Ed. Oliver H. Prior.
EETS, extra series, no. 110. London, 1913.

Cedrenus, Georgius. Compendium historiarum a mundo condito
usque ad Isaacium commenum imperatorem. Patrologia graeca,
CXXI.

Chaucer, Geoffrey. Complete works. Ed. F. N. Robinson. Boston
and New York, 1933.

Chronicon paschale: breviarum ab Adam. Patrologia graeca, XCII.

Chrysologus, Peter. Sermo CVII. Patrologia latina, LII.

Chrysostom, John. Enarratio in epistolam ad Hebraeos homilia
XXVII. Patrologia graeca, LXIII.

———. Expositio in Psalmos. Patrologia graeca, LV.

————. Homiliae in Matthaeum. Patrologia graeca, LVII.
Clapham, Henoch. A briefe of the Bible drawne into English poesy. Edinburgh, 1596.
Clark, Andrew, ed. The Shirburn ballads: 1585-1616. Oxford, 1907.
Clement of Alexandria. Paedagogus. Patrologia graeca, VIII.
————. Stromata. Patrologia graeca, VIII and IX.
Clement of Rome. Two letters concerning virginity. Ante-Nicene Christian library, XIV. Trans. B. L. Pratten. Edinburgh, 1874.
Comestor, Petrus. Historia scholastica. Patrologia latina, CXCVIII.
Cotelerius, J. B., ed. SS. patrum qui temporibus apostolicis floruerunt . . . opera. Amsterdam, 1724. 2 vols.
Cursor mundi. Ed. Richard Morris. EETS, original series, nos. 57 and 59. London, 1874-1875. 1 vol. in 2.
Cyprian. Heptateuchos. Ed. Rudolf Peiper. Corpus scriptorum ecclesiasticorum latinorum, XXIII. Vienna, 1891.
Cyril of Alexandria. De sancta et consubstantiali trinitate dialogus VI. Patrologia graeca, LXXV.
————. In librum Judicum homiliae VIII. Patrologia graeca, LXXV.
————. Pro sancta christianorum religione adversus libros athei Juliani. Patrologia graeca, LXXVI.
Damiani, Peter. Collectanea in vetus testamentum: in librum Judicum. Patrologia latina, CXLV.
————. Sermo LXVIII. Patrologia latina, CXLIV.
Diels, Hermann, and Walther Kranz, eds. Die Fragmente der Vorsokratiker. 5th ed. Berlin, 1934. 2 vols. Vol. I.
Diodati, John. Pious and learned annotations upon the Holy Bible. London, 1664.
Diodorus Siculus. Bibliotheca historica. Ed. F. Fogel. Leipzig, 1888-1906. 6 vols.
Diodorus of Tarsus. Fragmenta in librum Judicum. Patrologia graeca, XXXIII.
Donne, John. Biathanatos: a declaration of that paradoxe, or thesis, that selfe-homicide is not so naturally sinne, that it may never be otherwise. London, [1644].
————. Poems. Ed. H. J. C. Grierson. Oxford, 1912.
Downame, John. The Christian warfare. London, 1612.
Dramata sacra. Basel, 1547.
Du Bartas, Guillaume de Saluste. Works. Ed. Urban Tigner Holmes, et al. Chapel Hill, 1940. 3 vols.
Epictetus. Discourses. Trans. P. E. Matheson. In the Stoic and

Epicurean philosophers, ed. Whitney J. Oates. New York, 1940. Pp. 224-484.

Eugippius Africanus. Thesaurus ex sancti Augustini operibus. Patrologia latina, LXII.

Eusebius Pamphilius. Chronicorum canonum. Ed. Alfred Schoene. Berlin, 1866. 2 vols.

Eutychius of Alexandria. Annales. Patrologia graeca, CXI.

Fisher, John (Piscator). Analysis logica libri S. Lucae. London, 1597.

Fletcher, Phineas. Works. Ed. F. S. Boas. Cambridge, 1908. 2 vols.

Fuller, Nicholas. Miscellaneorum sacrorum libri duo, quintus & sextus. London, 1622.

Fuller, Thomas. A comment on the eleven first verses of the fourth chapter of S. Matthew's gospel concerning Christ's temptations, delivered in xii sermons. London, 1652.

Gascoigne, George. Works. Ed. J. W. Cunliffe. Cambridge, 1910. 2 vols.

Glasse, Salomon. Philologia sacra, qua totius SS. veteris et novi Testamenti scripturae tum stylus et literatura, tum sensus et genuinae interpretationis ratio expenditur libri quinque. Ed. Johannes Gothofredus Olearus. Frankfurt and Leipzig, 1691.

Glyca, Michaelis. Annales. Patrologia graeca, CLVIII.

Godefridus Admontensis. Homilia XLII. Patrologia latina, CLXXIV.

Godwin, Thomas. Synopsis antiquitatum Hebraicarum. Oxford, 1616.

Gower, John. English works. Ed. G. C. Macaulay. EETS, extra series, no. 82. London, 1901. 2 vols.

Gregory the Great. Epistolae. Patrologia latina, LXXVII.

———. Moralia. Patrologia latina, LXXV and LXXVI.

———. XL Homiliae in evangelia. Patrologia latina, LXXVI.

———. S. Paterii liber de expositione veteris ac novi Testamenti, de diversis libris S. Gregorii Magni concinnatus. Patrologia latina, LXXIX.

Gregory of Constantinople. Oratio IV: adversus Julianum. Patrologia graeca, XXXV.

———. Oratio XXI: in laudem Athanasii. Patrologia graeca, XXXV.

———. Poemata. Patrologia graeca, XXXVII.

Gregory of Nyssa. In sanctum pascha et de triduano festo resurrectionis Christi orationes quinque. Patrologia graeca, XLVI.

Grotius, Hugo. Annotationes in vetus Testamentum. Halle, 1775-1776. 3 vols. in 1.

Hall, Joseph. Contemplations upon the principal passages of the holie storie. London, 1615. Vol. III.

————. A plaine and familiar explication of the old and new Testaments. London, 1633.

Hamartolus, Georgius. Chronicon breve quod e diversis annalium scriptoribus et expositoribus decerpsit concinnavitque. Patrologia graeca, CX.

Harvey of Burgundy. Commentarii in epistolas Pauli. Patrologia latina, CLXXXI.

Haymo Halberstatensis. In Divini Pauli epistolas expositio: in epistolam ad Hebraeos. Patrologia latina, CXVII.

Hayne, Thomas. The general view of the Holy Scriptures: or, the times, places, and persons of the Holy Scriptures. London, 1640. First edition, 1607.

Herbert, George. Works. Ed. F. E. Hutchinson. Oxford, 1941.

Hugo of St. Victor. Adnotatiunculae in threnos Jeremiae secundum multiplicem sensum et primo secundum litteralem. Patrologia latina, CLXXV.

————. Allegoriae in vetus Testamentum. Patrologia latina, CLXXV.

Hutchins, Edward. Sampsons iavvbone against the spiritual Philistine: containing sundry Godly and Christian praiers, necessarie and conuenient for all estates and accasions. London, 1601.

Isidore of Pelusium. Epistolae de interpretatione divinae scripturae. Patrologia graeca, LXXVIII.

Isidore of Seville. De orte et obitu patrum. Patrologia latina, LXXXIII.

————. Etymologiae. Patrologia latina, LXXXII.

————. Mysticorum expositiones sacramentorum, seu quaestiones in vetus Testamentum: in librum Judicum. Patrologia latina, LXXXIII.

————. Sententiae. Patrologia latina, LXXXIII.

Ivo Carnotensis. Panormia, seu decretum. Patrologia latina, CLXI.

Jerome. Adversus Jovinianum. Patrologia latina, XXIII.

————. Commentarii in epistolam ad Ephesios. Patrologia latina, XXVI.

————. Commentarii in epistolam Philemonem. Patrologia latina, XXVI.

————. Commentarii in evangelium Matthaei. Patrologia latina, XXVI.

————. Commentarii in Ezechielem prophetam. Patrologia latina, XXV.

————. Divinae bibliothecae. Patrologia latina, XXVIII.

John of Salisbury. Policraticus, sive de nugis curialium et vestigiis philosophorum libri VIII. Ed. C. C. I. Webb. Oxford, 1909. 2 vols.

Josephus, Flavius. The famous and memorable works. Trans. Thomas Lodge. London, 1640.

———. Works, with an English translation. Ed. H. St. John Thackeray and Ralph Marcus. Loeb classical library. London and Cambridge, Mass., 1924. 8 vols.

Knox, John. Works. Ed. David Laing. Edinburgh, 1856. Vol. IV.

Lactantius. Divinarum institutionum liber quintus: de justitia. Patrologia latina, VI.

Lanfranc of Canterbury. In omnes Pauli epistolas commentarii cum glossula interjecta. Patrologia latina, CL.

Lapide, Cornelius à. Commentarius in Ioshue, Iudicum, Ruth. Antwerp, 1664.

Leo Magnus. Sermo LXXXIII. Patrologia latina, LIV.

Lightfoot, John. Whole works. Ed. J. R. Pitman. London, 1822-1825. 13 vols. Vol. VIII.

Liturgia Mozarabica. Patrologia latina, LXXXV.

Lombard, Peter. Collectanea in epistolas S. Pauli: in epistolam ad Hebraeos. Patrologia latina, CXCII.

Luca, Franciscus. In Lucam commentaria Scripturae sacrae cursus completus. Ed. J. D. Migne. Paris, 1862.

Ludus Coventriae, or the plaie called Corpus Christi. Ed. K. S. Bloch. EETS, extra series, no. 120. London, 1922.

Luther, Martin. Vorlesung über das Buch der Richter. Ed. Georg Buchwald. Leipzig, 1884.

Lydgate, John. Fall of princes. Ed. Henry Bergen. EETS, extra series, nos. 121, 122, 123. London, 1924. 1 vol. in 3.

———. Troy book. Ed. Henry Bergen. EETS, extra series, no. 97. London, 1906.

Lyly, John. Complete works. Ed. R. Warwick Bond. Oxford, 1902. 3 vols.

Marbecke, John. A booke of notes and commonplaces, with their expositions. London, 1581.

———. The lyues of holy sainctes, prophets, patriarches, and others, contayned in Holye Scripture. London, 1574.

Maurus, Rabanus. Commentarii in librum Judicum et Ruth. Patrologia latina, CVIII.

———. De universo. Patrologia latina, CXI.

———. Enarrationes in epistolas Beati Pauli. Patrologia latina, CXI and CXII.

———. Tractatus de anima. Patrologia latina, CX.

Maximus of Turin. Homilia cxv. Patrologia latina, LVII.

————. Sermo xxxvi. Patrologia latina, LVII.

Montanus, Benedictus Arias. De varia republica: sive, commentarius in librum Iudicum. Antwerp, 1592.

A most excellent and famous ditty of Sampson, judge of Israel. In Roxburghe ballads. Ed. Ballad society. Hertford, 1874. Vol. II.

Nashe, Thomas. Works. Ed. R. B. McKerrow. London, 1904. 5 vols.

Nilus Abbas. Peristeria. Patrologia graeca, LXXIX.

Oates, Whitney J., ed. The Stoic and Epicurean philosophers: the complete extant writings of Epicurus, Epictetus, Lucretius, Marcus Aurelius. New York, 1940.

Oecumenius of Tricca. Commentarius in epistolam Pauli ad Hebraeos. Patrologia graeca, CXIX.

Origen. Adnotationes in Judices. Patrologia graeca, XVII.

————. Commentarii in evangelium Joannis. Patrologia graeca, XIV.

————. In librum Judicum homiliae VIII. Patrologia graeca, XII.

Paradin, Claude. The true and lyuely historyke purtreatures of the woll Bible. Trans. Peter Derendel. Lyons, 1553.

Pareus, David. Opera theologica. Frankfurt, 1647. Vol. I.

Paschasius Radbertus. Expositio in Matthaeum. Patrologia latina, CXX.

Patrick, Simon. A commentary upon the books of Joshua, Judges, and Ruth. London, 1702.

Patten, William. The calender of Scripture. Whearin the Hebru, Challdian, Arabian, Phenician, Syrian, Persian, Greek and Latin names, of nations, cuntreys, men weemen, idols, cities, hils, riuers, & of oother places in the Holly Byble mentioned, by order of letters are set, and turned into oour English toong. London, 1575.

Paulinus of Nola. Epistola XXIII. Patrologia latina, LXI.

————. Poema XXIV. Patrologia latina, LXI.

Peter Martyr. See Vermigli, Pietro Martire.

Philastrius. Liber de haeresibus. Patrologia latina, XII.

Philip of Harveng. De obedientia clericorum. Patrologia latina, CCIII.

Plato. Dialogues. Trans. Benjamin Jowett. New York, 1937. 2 vols.

————. Opera. Ed. John Burnet. Oxford, n.d. Vol. I.

————. Res publica. Ed. John Burnet. Oxford, n.d.

Plutarch. Moralia. Ed. C. Hubert, W. Nachstädt, W. R. Paton,

M. Pohlenz, W. Sieveking, J. B. Titchener, I. Wegehaupt. Leipzig, 1925-1938. 4 vols.

Poole, Matthew. Synopsis criticorum. London, 1669.

Procopius of Gaza. Commentarii in Genesin. Patrologia graeca, LXXXVII.

————. Commentarii in Judices. Patrologia graeca, LXXXVII.

Prodromus, Theodorus. Epigrammata. Patrologia graeca, CXXXIII.

Prudentius. Dittochaeum. Patrologia latina, LX.

Prynne, William. Histrio-mastix. London, 1633.

Quarles, Francis. Complete works in verse and prose. Ed. Alexander B. Grosart. Chertsey worthies library. Edinburgh, 1880-1881. 3 vols.

Ravanellus, Petrus. Bibliotheca sacra, seu, thesaurus scripturae canonicae amplissimus. Geneva, 1650-1663. 3 vols.

Roberts, Francis. Clavis bibliorum. London, 1648.

Rogers, Richard. A commentary upon the whole booke of Judges. London, 1615.

Rollins, Hyder E., ed. The Pepys ballads. Cambridge, Mass., 1929. 8 vols.

Rothschild, James de, ed. Le mistere du viel Testament. Société des anciens textes français. Paris, 1882. Vol. IV.

Roxburghe ballads. Ed. Ballad society. Hertford, 1874. Vol. II.

Rupert of St. Heribert. Commentarii in Genesin. Patrologia latina, CLXVII.

————. De operibus spiritus sancti. Patrologia latina, CLXVII.

————. In librum Judicum commentarii. Patrologia latina, CLXVII.

————. In quatuor evangelistarum commentarii. Patrologia latina, CLXVII.

Salianus, Jacobus. Annales ecclesiastici veterus Testamenti. Cologne, 1620. Vol. II.

Sandys, Edwin. Sermons. Ed. John Ayre. Parker society publications. Cambridge, 1841.

Schmidt, Sebastian. In librum Judicum commentarius, in quo praeter diligentem textus explicationem, praecipuae quaestiones, et loci communes, quos vocant, ad singula capita, ac sub finem appendix chronologica, adduntur. Strassburg, 1684.

Severus, Sulpicius. Chronica. Ed. C. Halm. Corpus scriptorum ecclesiasticorum latinorum, I. Vienna, 1866.

Shakespeare, William. Works. Ed. George Lyman Kittredge. New York, 1936.

Spenser, Edmund. The faerie queene, Book v. Ed. Ray Heffner. Baltimore, 1936.

Strabo, Walafrid. Expositio in quatuor evangelia. Patrologia latina, CXIV.

————. Glossa ordinaria. Patrologia latina, CXIII.

Syncellus, Georgius. Chronographia. Ed. W. Dindorf. Corpus scriptorum historiae Byzantinae. Bonn, 1829. 2 vols.

Tertullian. De aetate apologetici Mosheimi disquisitio. Patrologia latina, I.

————. Liber de oratione. Patrologia latina, I.

Theodoret. Graecarum affectionum curatio. Patrologia graeca, LXXXIII.

————. Interpretatio epistolae ad Hebraeos. Patrologia graeca, LXXXII.

————.Quaestiones in Genesin. Patrologia graeca, LXXX.

————. Quaestiones in Judices. Patrologia graeca, LXXX.

————. Sermo VIII: de martyribus. Patrologia graeca, LXXXIII.

Theophylactus of Bulgaria. Expositio in epistolam ad Hebraeos. Patrologia graeca, CXXV.

Thomas Aquinas. Summa theologiae. Ed. Ottawa institute of medieval studies. Ottawa, 1942. Vol. III.

Thomas Cisterciensis. In cantica canticorum eruditissimi commentarii. Patrologia latina, CCVI.

Tirinus, Jacobus. In S. Scripturam duobus tomis comprehensus, quibus explicantur hoc primo post varia prolegomena vetus fere Testamentum. Venice, 1724.

Torniellus, Augustinus. Annales sacri et profani. Cologne, 1622-1626. 2 vols. in 1.

Tostadus, Alfonsus. Opera. Venice, 1728. Vol. I.

Vaughan, Edward. Ten introductions how to read all the books in the Holy Bible. London, 1594.

Vermigli, Pietro Martire (Peter Martyr). In librum Iudicum commentarii doctissimi, cum tractatione perutile rerum et locorum. Zurich, 1571.

Wastell, Simon. Microbiblion, or the Bibles epitome. London, 1629.

Zonaras, Joannes. Annales. Patrologia graeca, CXXXIV.

II. EDITIONS OF MILTON

Complete poetical works. Ed. William Vaughn Moody. Boston and New York, 1899.

Facsimile of the manuscript of Milton's minor poems preserved in the library of Trinity college, Cambridge. Ed. W. A. Wright. Cambridge, 1899.

Paradise regain'd, a poem in IV books, to which is added Samson agonistes. London, 1671.

Paradise regained, the minor poems, and Samson agonistes complete and arranged chronologically. Ed. Merritt Y. Hughes. New York, 1937.

Poetical works. Ed. David Masson. London, 1890. 3 vols.

Poetical works. Ed. Henry J. Todd. London, 1809. 7 vols. First edition, 1801.

Poetical works, with notes of various authors. Ed. Thomas Newton. London, 1749-1761. 3 vols.

Samson agonistes. Ed. A. J. Church. London, 1872.

Samson agonistes. Ed. A. W. Verity. Pitt press series. Cambridge, Mass., 1932. [First edition, 1912.]

Samson agonistes and English sonnets, with introduction and notes. Ed. H. M. Perceval. London, 1931. [First edition, 1890.]

The student's Milton. Ed. Frank Allen Patterson. Rev. ed. New York, 1933.

Works. Ed. Frank Allen Patterson, et al. New York, 1931-1938. 18 vols. in 21. [The "Columbia edition".]

III. SELECTED SECONDARY SOURCES

Barker, Arthur. Milton's schoolmasters. MLR, xxxii (1937), 517-36.

Baum, Paul Franklin. Samson agonistes again. PMLA, xxxvi (1921), 354-71.

[Beerbohm, Max.] Samson agonistes and Zaza. Saturday review of literature, lxxxix (1900), 489.

Belloc, Hilaire. Milton. London, 1935.

Boughner, Daniel C. Milton's Harapha and renaissance comedy. ELH, xi (1944), 297-306.

Brewer, Wilmon. Two Athenian models for Samson agonistes. PMLA, xlii (1927), 910-20.

Brooke, Stopford A. Milton. Classical writers series. New York, 1899.

Bush, Douglas. The renaissance and English humanism. Toronto, 1939.

Campbell, Lily B. The Christian muse. Huntington library bulletin, October 1935, pp. 29-70.

Clark, Evert M. Milton's conception of Samson. University of Texas studies in English, viii (1928), 88-99.

————. Milton's earlier Samson. University of Texas studies in English, VII (1927), 144-54.

Coleridge, Samuel Taylor. Seven lectures on Shakespeare. Ed. J. Payne Collier. London, 1856.

Corcoran, Sister Mary Irma. Milton's Paradise with reference to the hexaemeral background. Catholic university of America dissertation, 1945.

Cory, Herbert E. Spenser, the school of the Fletchers, and Milton. University of California publications. Berkeley, 1912.

Curry, Walter C. Samson agonistes yet again. Sewanee review, XXXII (1924), 336-52.

Darbishire, Helen. Review of J. R. P. Mody's Vondel and Milton. RES, XIX, 330.

Deutsch, Alfred H. Some scholastic elements in Paradise lost. University of Illinois dissertation, 1945.

Dunster, Charles. Considerations on Milton's early reading. London, 1800.

Edmundson, George. Milton and Vondel: a curiosity of literature. London, 1885.

Ellis-Fermor, Una. The frontiers of drama. London, 1946.

Finney, Gretchen L. Chorus in Samson agonistes. PMLA, LVIII (1943), 649-64.

Fletcher, Harris F. Milton and Rashi. JEGP, XXVII (1928), 300-17.

————. Milton's use of biblical quotations. JEGP, XXVI (1927), 145-65.

————. The use of the Bible in Milton's prose. University of Illinois studies in language and literature, XIV. Urbana, 1929.

————. Milton's rabbinical readings. Urbana, 1930.

Gilbert, Allan H. Review of J. H. Hanford's Samson agonistes and Milton in old age. MLN, XLI (1926), 266f.

————. The theological basis of Satan's rebellion and the function of Abdiel in Paradise lost. MP, XL (1942-1943), 19-42.

Gray, F. Campbell. Milton's counterpoint: classicism and romanticism in the poetry of John Milton. Sewanee review, XLIII (1935), 134-45.

Grierson, Sir Herbert J. C. Milton and Wordsworth: poets and prophets: a study of their reactions to political events. Cambridge, 1937.

————. A note upon the Samson agonistes of John Milton and Samson of heilige wraeck by Joost van den Vondel. In Mélanges . . . Baldensperger. Paris, 1930.

Hanford, James Holly. The chronology of Milton's private studies. PMLA, xxxvi (1921), 251-314.

————. Milton and the return to humanism. SP, xvi (1919), 126-47.

————. A Milton handbook. Third edition revised. New York, 1944.

————. Samson agonistes and Milton in old age. In Studies in Shakespeare, Milton, and Donne by members of the English department of the university of Michigan. University of Michigan publications in language and literature, i. New York and London, 1925.

————. That shepherd, who first taught the chosen seed: a note upon Milton's Mosaic inspiration. University of Toronto quarterly, viii, 403-19.

————. The temptation motive in Milton. SP, xv (1918), 176-94.

Harding, Davis P. Milton and the renaissance Ovid. Illinois studies in language and literature, xxx. Urbana, 1946.

Hartwell, Kathleen. Lactantius and Milton. Cambridge, Mass., 1929.

Jebb, Sir Richard C. Samson agonistes and the Hellenic drama. Proceedings of the British academy, iii (1907-1908), 341-48.

Johnson, Samuel. Works, with an essay on his life and genius by Arthur Murphy. London, 1801. 12 vols.

Kelley, Maurice. Milton's debt to Wolleb's Compendium theologiae Christianae. PMLA, l, 156-65.

Knowlton, E. C. Causality in Samson agonistes. MLN, xxxvii (1922), 333-39.

Kreipe, Christian E. Milton's Samson agonistes. Studien zur englischen Philologie, lxx. Halle, 1926.

Krouse, F. Michael. Review of Davis P. Harding's Milton and the renaissance Ovid. MLN, lxii (1947), 135-38.

Larson, Martin A. The modernity of Milton: a theological and philosophical interpretation. Chicago, 1927.

Legouis, Emile. A history of English literature: the middle ages and the renaissance. Revised edition. New York, 1935.

Lovejoy, A. O. Milton and the paradox of the fortunate fall. ELH, iv (1937), 161-79.

McColley, Grant. Milton's Ariel. N&Q, clxxvi, 45.

————. Milton's battle in heaven and Rupert of St. Heribert. Speculum, xvi (1941), 230-35.

Menzies, W. Milton: the last poems. Essays and studies by members of the English association, xxiv (1939), 80-113.

Mody, Jehangir R. P. Vondel and Milton. Bombay, 1942.
Morley, Edith, ed. Henry Crabbe Robinson on books and their writers. London, 1938. 2 vols.
Nicolson, Marjorie H. Milton and the Conjectura cabbalistica. PQ, VI (1927), 1-18.
Parker, William Riley. The Greek spirit in Milton's Samson agonistes. Essays and studies by members of the English association, xx (1934), 21-44.
————. The kommos of Milton's Samson agonistes. SP, xxxii (1935), 240-44.
————. Milton's debt to Greek tragedy in Samson agonistes. Baltimore, 1937.
————. On Milton's early literary program. MP, xxxiii (1935), 49-53.
Pattison, Mark. Milton. English men of letters series. London and New York, 1902.
Pope, Elizabeth Marie. Paradise regained: the tradition and the poem. Baltimore, 1947.
Pritchard, John P. The fathers of the church in the works of John Milton. Classical journal, xxxiii (1937-1938), 79-87.
Raleigh, Sir Walter. Milton. London, 1914.
Ramsay, Robert L. Morality themes in Milton's poetry. SP, xv (1918), 123-58.
Richardson, Jonathan. Explanatory notes and remarks on Milton's Paradise lost, with the life of the author, and a discourse on the poem. London, 1734.
Saurat, Denis. La Cabale et la philosophie de Milton. Revue des études juives, LXXIII (1921), 1-13.
————. Milton: man and thinker. New York, 1925.
Scott-Craig, T. S. K. Milton's use of Wolleb and Ames. MLN, LV, 403-7.
Southey, Robert. Studies in the literature of northern Europe. London, 1883.
Svendson, Kester. Milton and the encyclopedias of science. SP, xxxix (1942), 303-27.
Thompson, E. N. S. Essays on Milton. New Haven, 1914.
Tillyard, E. M. W. Milton. London, 1930.
Tupper, James W. The dramatic structure of Samson agonistes. PMLA, xxxv (1920), 375-89.
Tuve, Rosemond. Elizabethan and metaphysical imagery: Renaissance poetic and twentieth-century critics. Chicago, 1947.
Whiting, George W. Milton's literary milieu. Chapel Hill, 1939.
Willey, Basil. The seventeenth-century background: studies in

the thought of the age in relation to poetry and religion. London, 1933.
Williams, Arnold. Milton and the renaissance commentaries on Genesis. MP, xxxvii (1939-1940), 263-78.
———. Renaissance commentaries on Genesis and some elements of the theology of Paradise lost. PMLA, lvi (1941), 151-64.
Woodhouse, A. S. P. Milton and his age. University of Toronto quarterly, v, 130-39.
Wordsworth, William. Prose works. Ed. Alexander B. Grosart. London, 1876. 3 vols.
Young, G. M. Milton and Harrington. TLS, 9 January 1937, p. 28.

IV. MISCELLANEOUS WORKS OF REFERENCE

Albright, William F. From the stone age to Christianity: monotheism and the historical process. Baltimore, 1940.
Allacci, Lione. Drammaturgia. Venice, 1755.
Allen, Don Cameron. Latin literature of the renaissance. MLQ, ii (1941), 403-20.
Alzog, Johannes. Grundriss der Patrologie oder der ältern christlichen Literaturgeschichte. Freiburg im Breisgau, 1888.
Amatucci, A. G. Storia della letteratura latina Cristiana. Bari, 1929.
Aulén, Gustaf. Christus victor: an historical study of the three main types of the idea of the atonement. Trans. A. G. Hebert. Society for promoting Christian knowledge. London and New York, 1931.
Ayer, Joseph C. A source book for ancient church history from the apostolic age to the close of the conciliar period. New York, 1913.
Bardenhewer, Otto. Patrologie. Freiburg im Breisgau, 1910.
Barrera y Leirado, Cayetano Alberto de la. Catálogo bibliográfico y biográfico del teatro antiguo español, desde sus orígenes hasta mediados del siglo xviii. Madrid, 1860.
Blount, Edward. Glossographia. London, 1681.
Bolte, Johannes, ed. Coligny, Gustaf Adolf, Wallenstein: drei zeitgenössische lateinische Dramen von Rhodius, Narssius, Vernulaeus. Bibliothek des litterarischen Vereins in Stuttgart, cclxxx. Leipzig, 1933.
Bradner, Leicester. A check-list of original neo-Latin dramas by continental writers printed before 1650. PMLA, lviii (1945), 621-33.

Campbell, James M. The Greek fathers. Our debt to Greece and Rome, xxxiv. New York, 1929.

Cook, Albert S. Biblical quotation in Old English prose writers. London and New York, 1898.

Craig, Hardin, et al. Recent literature of the renaissance. SP, xvi (1919), xvii (1920), xix (1922)-xliii (1946).

Dilthey, Wilhelm. Die Entstehung der Hermeneutik. In Gesammelte Schriften. Ed. Georg Misch. Leipzig and Berlin, 1924. Vol. v.

Driver, Samuel R. An introduction to the literature of the old Testament. International theological library. New York, 1891.

Du Cange, Charles du Fresne. Glossarium ad scriptores mediae et infimae graecitatis. Lyons, 1688. Vol. i.

————. Glossarium ad scriptores mediae et infimae latinitatis. Paris, 1678.

Dummelow, J. R., ed. A commentary on the Holy Bible by various writers. New York, 1938.

Ellendt, Friedrich. Lexicon Sophocleum. Königsberg, 1835. Vol. i.

Erith, L. E. P. Judges. In A new commentary on Holy Scripture. Ed. C. Gore, H. L. Goudge, and A. Guillaume. New York, 1929.

Farrar, Frederic. History of interpretation. Bampton lectures. London, 1886.

Fletcher, Harris F. Contributions to a Milton bibliography: 1800-1930. University of Illinois studies in language and literature, xvi. Urbana, 1931.

Frazer, Sir James G. Folk-lore in the old Testament: studies in comparative religion, legend, and law. London, 1919. 3 vols.

Gilbert, George H. Interpretation of the Bible: a short history. New York, 1908.

Ginzberg, Louis. The legends of the Jews. Trans. Henrietta Szold. Philadelphia, 1910-1938. 7 vols.

Goedeke, Karl. Grundriss zur Geschichte der deutschen Dichtung aus den Quellen. Dresden, 1886. Vol. ii.

Goodspeed, Edgar J. A history of early Christian literature. Chicago, 1942.

Harbage, Alfred. Annals of English drama: 975-1700. Philadelphia, 1940.

Havens, Raymond Dexter. The influence of Milton on English poetry. Cambridge, Mass., 1922.

Kittel, G., ed. Theologisches Wörterbuch zum neuen Testament. Stuttgart, 1933. Vol. i.

Labriolle, Pierre de. Histoire de la litterature latine chrétienne. Paris, 1920.

Lancaster, Henry Carrington. A history of French dramatic literature in the seventeenth century: part I, the pre-classical period, 1610-1634. Baltimore and Paris, 1929. 2 vols.

Lanson, Gustave. Esquisse d'une histoire de la tragédie française. New York, 1920.

Lebegue, Raymond. Bibliothèque littéraire de la renaissance. Paris, 1929. Vol. xvii: la tragédie religieuse en France.

Lewis, Clive Staples. The allegory of love. London, 1936.

Liddell, Henry George, and Robert Scott. A Greek-English lexicon. Revised edition, ed. Sir Henry Stuart Jones. Oxford, 1940. 2 vols.

Linwood, W. A lexicon to Aeschylus. London, 1847.

Lipenus, Martinus. Bibliotheca realis theologica omnium materiarum, rerum, et titulorum, in vniuerso SS. theologiae studio occurrentium. Frankfort am Main, 1685. 2 vols.

Masson, David. The life of John Milton, narrated in connexion with the political, ecclesiastical, and literary history of his time. London and New York, 1871-1894. 7 vols.

Matthias, A. Lexicon Euripideum. Leipzig, 1841.

Moore, George F. A critical and exegetical commentary on Judges. New York, 1895.

Ottley, Robert L. Aspects of the old Testament, considered in eight lectures delivered before the university of Oxford. Bampton lectures. London and New York, 1897.

Owst, G. R. Literature and the pulpit in medieval England. Cambridge, 1933.

Patterson, Frank Allen, and F. R. Fogle. An index to the Columbia edition of the works of John Milton. New York, 1940. 2 vols.

Peters, John R. The religion of the Hebrews. Cambridge, Mass., 1923.

Pinto, V. de Sola. The English renaissance: 1510-1688. Introductions to English literature. Ed. Bonamy Dobree. New York, 1938.

Pollard, Alfred W., and G. R. Redgrave. A short-title catalogue. London, 1926.

Raby, F. J. E. History of Christian-Latin poetry from the beginnings to the close of the middle ages. Oxford, 1927.

Renwick, W. L., and Harold Orton. The beginnings of English literature. Introductions to English literature. Ed. Bonamy Dobree. New York, 1940.

Riccoboni, Luigi. Histoire du théâtre italien. Paris, 1728.

Rollins, Hyder E. An analytical index to the ballad-entries in the register of the company of the stationers of London: 1557-1709. SP, xxi (1924), 1-324.

Rumpel, J. Lexicon Pindaricum. Leipzig, 1883.

Shorey, Paul. Φύσις, Μελέτη, Ἐπιστήμη. Transactions and proceedings of the American philological association, xl (1909), 185-201.

Smith, Henry Preserved. Essays in biblical interpretation. Boston, 1921.

Stevens, David H. Reference guide to Milton from 1800 to the present day. Chicago, 1930.

Thesaurus linguae latinae. Leipzig, 1900-1940. 9 vols. Vol. i.

Thompson, E. N. S. John Milton: a topical bibliography. New Haven and London, 1916.

Walch, Johann Georg. Bibliotheca theologica selecta litterariis adnotationibus instructa. Jena, 1757-1765.

Williams, Arnold. Commentaries on Genesis as a basis for hexaemeral material in the literature of the late renaissance. SP, xxxiv (1937), 191-208.

Index

Abel, 29
Abelard, Peter, 55 and n., 56, 58,
106n., 124
Abraham, 29, 44n., 116
Adam, 59 and n., 125
Admiral's Theatre, 87
Ælfric, 47n., 50, 93n.
Aeschylus, 8n., 9n., 10, 111n.
Agon, concept of life as, 109-18,
130, 133
Agonistes, significance of, as epi-
thet, 108-18, 124, 130
Alanus ab Insulis, 49, 54n., 96
Albright, W. F., 22 and n., 23
and n., 24n.
Allacci, Lione, 86n.
Allegory, as form of biblical inter-
pretation, 31, 39-44, 45, 49-
54, 64, 68-70, 77-79, 81, 85,
119-24, 130
Allen, D. C., vii
Ambrose, 18n., 35 and n., 36n.,
40 and n., 65, 76, 94 and n.,
103, 114n., 121
Anagoge, as form of biblical inter-
pretation, 54, 72, 88
Andrewes, Lancelot, 115 and n.
Antaeus, 130
Aquinas, Thomas, 49, 94 and n.,
96, 124
Ariosto, 123
Aristotle, 8, 84, 105n., 111, 131
Artemis, 45
Ashtaroth, 92
Athanasius, 18n., 36
Atterbury, Francis, 7
Atto of Vercelli, 47 and n.
Augustine, 18n., 36n., 37, 39, 40-
42, 45, 49, 63-65, 94 and n.,
114, 116n., 117, 130n.
Aulén, Gustaf, 114-15
Auto de Sanson, 86

Baal, 92
Barac, 23, 29, 47
Barker, A., 18n.

Barrera y Leirado, A. de la, 86n.
Basil, 18n.
Baum, P. F., 8n., 14n.
Bede, 43n., 93n., 106n., 115 and
n.
Beerbohm, M., 8n.
Belial, 102
Belloc, H., 13n.
Bible, "Breeches" ("Geneva" Bi-
ble), 74n., 76n., 77n., 85n.
Bible, Esther, 12, 29; Hebrews,
29, 33, 36, 47, 49 and n., 98,
130; Job, 7, 44n., 81, 116;
Judges, *passim*, Deuteronomic
redaction of, 24, historical back-
ground of, 23, origin of in folk-
lore, 22-23, source of Samson
tradition in, 22-29, story of
Samson in, 24-28; Revelations,
124; Timothy, 118
Biblical interpretation, *see* Literal-
ism, Allegory, Anagoge, Tropol-
ogy, Rationalism
Boccaccio, Giovanni, 60, 85
Bolte, J., 86n.
Bonfrerius, Jacobus, 64, 69, 76
and n., 78n., 128n.
Bonus, Jacobus, 130n.
Boughner, D., 13n., 14n., 129
Bradner, L., 86n.
Brenz, Johann, 63, 70, 74n.,
83n., 85, 96
Brewer, W., 10n.
Brooke, S. A., 13n.
Bucer, Martin, 18n.
Bullinger, Henry, 18n., 74n., 75,
76 and n., 77 and n., 96
Burton, Robert, 73 and n., 103
Bush, D., 11n., 16n.
Buxtorf, Johannes, 18n.

Cabala, 16n.
Cajetan (Tomasso de Vio Gaeta-
no), 64, 66, 74n., 75-76, 102
Calfhill, James, 68 and n., 119

154 Index

Calvin, Jean, 18n., 74 and n., 83, 96
Cameron, A., viii
Campbell, L. B., 11n.
Canaanites, 23
Capell, Louis, 18n.
Cassianus, 76
Caxton, William, 73n.
Cedrenus, Georgius, 47n., 93n.
Chaucer, Geoffrey, 59 and n., 60, 72, 73n., 78
Christ, *see* Allegory, Samson as figure of Christ
Chronicon Paschale, 34, 45, 46n., 64, 93n., 106n.
Chrysologus, Peter, 116n.
Chrysostom, John, 18n., 36, 76, 115 and n.
Church, A. J., 5n.
Clapham, Henoch, 68, 69n., 119
Clark, E. M., 13n., 14
Clement of Alexandria, 18n., 34n., 93n.
Clement of Rome, 34 and n.
Coleridge, S. T., 9
Collier, J. P., 9n.
Comestor, Petrus, 32, 46n., 47 and n., 55n., 65, 93n., 106n.
Congregazione dell' Oratoria della Madonna della Fava, 86
Coningh, Abraham de, 87
Corcoran, Sister Mary Irma, 17n.
Cory, H., 13n.
Cumberland, Richard, 8 and n.
Curry, W. C., 8n.
Cursor Mundi, 58, 59, 60, 72
Cyprian, 18n., 34n., 46n., 106n., 114
Cyril of Alexandria, 34n., 36n., 38n., 93n., 94 and n.

Dagon, 28, 52, 68n., 89, 90, 94, 96, 98n.
Dalila, 8, 13 and n., 27-28, 38, 43, 51n., 52, 55, 56, 57, 58-61, 66, 69, 76-77, 84, 97, 100, 101-3, 122-23, 127-28, 131

Damiani, Peter, 51 and n., 121, 122n.
Daniel, 37
Darbishire, H., 6n.
David, 29, 36, 44n., 49n., 57n., 73
De La Haye, Jean, 63, 64n., 69, 71n., 76n.
De Lyra, Nicholas, 50n., 64, 66, 68 and n., 71n., 74n., 77 and n., 121n.
Diels, H., 110n.
Dilthey, W., 31n.
Diodati, John, 18n., 68, 69n., 120, 122
Diodorus of Tarsus, 36n.
Diodorus Siculus, 18n., 44
Donne, John, 15, 68, 69n., 74n., 75, 78
Downame, John, 115, 116n.
Driver, S. R., 22n.
Du Bartas, G. de S., 6, 65n.
Dummelow, J. R., 22n.
Dunster, Charles, 6, 108

Edelstein, L., vii
Edmundson, G., 6 and n.
Eli, 23, 44n.
Ellis-Fermor, U., 8n.
Enoch, 29, 44n.
Epictetus, 113
Erasmus, 18n.
Erith, L. E. P., 22n.
Esther, Book of, *see* Bible
Estius, 71n.
Eugippius Africanus, 42n.
Euripides, 8n., 9n., 10, 111n.
Eusebius of Caesarea, 44 and n.
Eutychius of Alexandria, 46n., 55n.
Ezra, 32

Fabricius, Andreas, 86
Farnham, W., 11n.
Ficino, M., 10n.
Finney, G. L., 10n.
Fisher, John, 115 and n.
Fletcher, H. F., 11n., 18 and n.

Fletcher, Phineas, 73n., 103
Fogle, F. R., 32n.
Frazer, J. G., 22
Fuller, Thomas, 115, 116n.

Gascoigne, George, 73 and n., 103
Genealogia Christi, 68, 69n.
Giattini, Vincento, 86
Gideon, 23, 29, 49n., 98
Gilbert, A. H., vii, 17n., 86n.
Ginzberg, L., 22
Glasse, Salomon, 64, 65n.
Glyca, Michaelis, 64n., 65, 93n.
Godefridus Admontensis, 55 and n., 56
Godwin, Thomas, 74n.
Goedeke, K., 86n.
Gohn, E. S., vii
Gore, C., 22n.
Gosse, E., 6n.
Goudge, H. L., 22n.
Gower, John, 60, 72, 78
Gray, F. C., 11n.
Gregory the Great, 18n., 38 and n., 41n., 83, 106 and n., 121 and n.
Gregory Nazianzen, 19, 85
Grieck, Claude de, 87
Grierson, H. J. C., 6n., 13n., 14n., 17n.
Grosart, A. B., 12n.
Grotius, Hugo, 18n., 93n.
Groto, Luigi, 86n.
Guillaume, A., 22n.

Hall, Joseph, 68, 69n., 74n., 75, 76n., 77 and n., 83 and n., 84, 85n., 105
Hamartia, 38, 83
Hamartolus, Georgius, 47 and n., 55n., 93n.
Hanford, J. H., 6, 12 and n., 14n., 18n.
Harapha, 8, 13 and n., 14n., 94n., 95, 127, 128-30, 130n., 131
Harbage, A., 86n.
Harding, D. P., 10n.
Hartwell, K., 18n.

Harvey of Burgundy, 48
Havens, R. D., vii, 3, 7n.
Haymo Halberstatensis, 47 and n.
Hayne, Thomas, 69, 74n., 75, 76n., 94 and n., 119
Hebrews, Epistle to the, *see* Bible
Herbert, George, 68, 69n., 119
Hercules, 31, 44, 45 and n., 57, 59 and n., 72, 73, 78, 79, 85, 87, 111, 130 and n.
Hesiod, 5
Hillel, 32
Horace, 5
Horus-Ra, 45n.
Hughes, M. Y., 5n., 13n., 15, 16, 45n., 109
Hugo of St. Victor, 54, 55n., 106n.
Hume, Patrick, 5n.
Hurd, Richard, 3, 9
Hutchins, Edward, 74n.
Hybris, 38, 83

Idatius of Chaves, 34
Ignatius of Antioch, 116
Irenaeus, 18n., 114, 116
Isaac, 29, 44n.
Isidore of Seville, 18n., 34, 42 and n., 43 and n., 65, 93n., 114, 116 and n.
Isocrates, 112 and n.
Ivo Carnotensis, 48n.

Jacob, 29, 44n., 52, 53
Jair, 23
Jebb, R., 9, 11, 82
Jephthah, 23, 29, 47, 49n., 98
Jeremiah, 54
Jerome, 18n., 33, 38, 40n., 42n., 45n., 63, 65, 76, 115 and n.
Job, Book of, *see* Bible
Johnson, Samuel, 7, 8 and n., 125
Jonson, Ben, 9n.
Joseph, 29
Josephus, Flavius, 6, 32 and n., 33, 38, 46n., 63, 65, 76, 81, 83
Joshua, 44n.

Index

Samson, as agent of God impelled
by the Holy Spirit, 37, 74, 79,
89, 93-97, 132; as betrayed
lover, 31, 57-61, 72-74, 76-77,
84, 100-4; as counterpart of
Hercules, 31, 44-45, 59, 78-
79, 85, 130; as example of lust-
fulness, 31, 34-35, 37, 58-61,
70-71, 72-74, 76-77; as fallen
hero, 37-38, 75, 84, 88-89, 99,
103-4; as historical personage,
23-24, 32, 34, 47, 65-66, 78;
as saint, 29-30, 31, 36-37, 47-
49, 55, 61, 74-75, 79, 97-99,
108, 130-31; as tragic hero, 12,
14-15, 38, 55, 58-62, 78, 82-
88, 97; as tribal folk-hero, 22-
24, 29-30, 39; as type of Christ,
31, 40-44, 50-52, 55-56, 57,
62, 68-70, 77-79, 85, 119-24,
130, 132-33; repentance of,
77, 79, 104-6
Samson Agonistes, see Milton
Samuel, 23, 29, 36, 49n.
Sandrinelli, Bernardo, 86
Sandys, Edwin, 68 and n.
Sanxon, 85, 86n.
Sarah, 29
Satan, 43, 76, 102, 118, 125,
128, 129, 130, 132
Saurat, D., 13n., 16n.
Schmidt, Sebastian, 67, 72, 75
and n., 76n., 77 and n., 106n.
Scott-Craig, T. S. K., 114n.
Scotus, John Duns, 124
Seneca, 5, 113, 114
Septuagint, 32, 34n.
Serarius, 63, 64, 66, 76, 77, 78
Shafer, R., viii
Shakespeare, William, 3, 9n., 72,
78, 103
Shirburn Ballads, 103n.
Shorey, P., 112 and n.
Socrates, 110, 111, 112n.
Solomon, 73
Sophocles, 8n., 9 and n., 10 and
n., 82, 85, 111n.

Southey, R., 6
Spangenberg, Wolfert, 86n.
Spenser, Edmund, *The Faerie
Queene,* 3, 73, 78, 103, 123,
124
Strabo, Walafrid, 50 and n., 51,
106, 121
Sulpicius Severus, 18n., 33n.,
46n., 76, 93n.
Svendsen, K., 16n.
Sylvester, Joshua, 6
Syncellus, Georgius, 45n.

Tasso, 123
Tertullian, 114, 116n.
Theodoret, 18n., 36 and n., 37,
38, 52, 63, 65, 96, 116
Theodorus Prodromus, *see* Prodro-
mus
Theophylactus of Bulgaria, 47 and
n., 55n.
Thesaurus Linguae Latinae, 114n.
Thomas Cisterciensis, 54, 55n.
Thompson, E. N. S., 11n.
Tillyard, E. M. W., 3, 13n., 14n.
Timothy, Epistle to, *see* Bible
Tirinus, Jacobus, 64, 65n., 69,
71n., 76n., 78n.
Todd, H. J., 5n., 6, 8n., 13n.,
17n., 69n., 108n.
Torniellus, Augustinus, 64, 65 and
n., 93n., 106n.
Tostadus, Alfonsus, 64 and n., 66
*Tragedie Nouuelle de Samson le
Fort,* 87
Tremellius, Immanuel, 34n., 95n.
Tropology, as form of biblical in-
terpretation, 70-72, 88-89
Tsikal, 23
Tupper, J. W., 8n.

Vaughan, Edward, 75n.
Vergil, 5
Verity, A. W., 5n., 6n., 13n., 108,
132
Vermigli, Pietro Martire (Peter
Martyr), 63, 64, 66, 93n.
Vigilius, 35, 103